Curriculum

AS CONVERSATION

ARTHUR N. APPLEBEE

· · · ·

Curriculum

AS CONVERSATION

**TRANSFORMING TRADITIONS OF
TEACHING AND LEARNING**

THE UNIVERSITY OF CHICAGO PRESS / CHICAGO AND LONDON

The University of Chicago Press, Chicago 60637
The University of Chicago Press, Ltd., London
© 1996 by The University of Chicago
All rights reserved. Published 1996
Printed in the United States of America
05 04 03 02 01   00 99   2 3 4 5

ISBN: 0-226-02121-1 (cloth)
        0-226-02123-8 (paper)

Library of Congress Cataloging-in-Publication Data

Applebee, Arthur N.
    Curriculum as conversation : transforming traditions of teaching
and learning / Arthur N. Applebee.
        p.   cm.
    Includes bibliographical references and index.
    ISBN 0-226-02121-1 (cloth : alk. paper). — ISBN 0-226-02123-8
    1. Education—United States—Curricula.   2. Curriculum change—
United States.   3. Curriculum planning—United States.   I. Title.
LB1570.P67   1996
375'.00973—dc20   95-42694
                                                              CIP

contents

• • • •

ACKNOWLEDGMENTS · · · ·

For the past eight years, I have been involved in a series of studies of English instruction in general and the teaching of literature in particular as it is typically practiced in American schools. Carried out under the sponsorship of the National Research Center on Literature Teaching and Learning at the University at Albany, State University of New York, and funded primarily by the U.S. Department of Education, these studies have given me an opportunity to explore in considerable depth the successes and failures of our schools today. Detailed reports on these studies are available elsewhere, but the present volume gives me the opportunity to stand away from these details and ask *why* we have ended up with schools and colleges that, while not particularly exciting places for teachers or students, have passed virtually unchanged through wave after wave of educational reform. The answer, I believe, lies in the ways we have thought about cultural traditions of knowing and doing, about what students should know, and about how to embed that knowledge in specific curricula. I develop this argument, grounded in the experiences of my own studies as well as those of many other scholars and teachers, in the present volume.

This book draws for particular examples on a series of studies of how teachers make decisions about their own curricula. Bob Burroughs and Anita Stevens were project staff members for those studies, and their careful observations and analyses contributed to the conceptualization of curriculum that underlies my argument here. Special thanks are also due to Judith A. Langer, who pushed me to write (and eventually to rewrite) this book even when the topic seemed too slippery and the time seemed too short; to Alan C. Purves, who always pushes me to draw on a wider universe of scholars and critics; and to the many other colleagues at the Center and around the country whose work has enriched my thinking.

The ideas developed in this book have evolved over a number of years. Earlier versions of some of my arguments have appeared in working papers from the National Research Center on Literature Teaching and Learning (Applebee 1993a; Applebee, Burroughs, and Stevens 1994) and in Applebee 1994.

This work was supported in part by grant number R117G10015, sponsored by the Office of Research, Office of Educational Research and Improvement, U.S. Department of Education; by the University at Albany, State University of New York; and by the Rockefeller Foundation. I am indebted to all three. However, the opinions expressed do not necessarily reflect the positions or policies of the funding agencies, and no official endorsement should be inferred.

A. N. A.
Villa Serbelloni
Bellagio, Italy

Introduction: The Role
of Tradition

I begin with tradition: what we mean by it, how it shapes our individual and cultural lives, and, most of all, its relationships to what and how we teach. I will argue that the power of education is intimately bound up in the social and cultural traditions within which education is set. These traditions enable and transform the minds of individuals raised within them, and are in turn themselves transformed by those same individuals. Traditions change as the circumstances that surround them change; in that way they preserve their power to guide the present and the future as well as to reflect the past.

The rhetoric of educational reform, however, has distorted the nature of tradition and its relationship to education. Tradition has been construed as antiprogressive, out of date. It is attacked for preserving the status quo, resisting reform, obstructing social justice.[1] Reinforcing these connotations, conservative educationists have turned to tradition as a source of common values, social stability, and intellectual attainment (see Adler, Van Doren, Bennett, and Bloom).[2] Matthew Arnold's title *Culture and Anarchy* (1867) starkly encapsulated the choice as he saw it, and his rhetoric continues to echo through our contemporary debates.

But that characterization of education and tradition is simplistic. In particular, in this book I will argue that traditions are the knowledge-in-action out of which we construct our

---

1. I have been as guilty as any in playing off this dichotomy; e.g., Applebee, *Tradition and Reform in the Teaching of English* (1974).
2. I am using common usage here; in fact Adler (1940), Bennett (1988), Bloom (1987), and Van Doren (1943) are advocates of a continuing "liberal education" tradition that is, paradoxically, conservative in its emphases.

realities as we know and perceive them, and that to honor such traditions we must reconstrue our curriculum to focus on knowledge-in-action rather than knowledge-out-of-context. Traditions in this sense provide *culturally constituted tools* for understanding and reforming the world, tools of which we, Janus-like, are both heir and progenitor. As we move through life, we learn to draw upon many different traditions that provide alternative, often complementary, ways of knowing and doing—of defining the world and of existing within it.

I write these words sitting at a window at the Villa Serbelloni, in the Lake District of northern Italy, surrounded by traditions. The villa walls are three feet thick, built out of layers of plaster and rubble using techniques that go back thousands of years. My study is in a building that has been a church, a monastery, a private home. It still houses a chapel. Out my window are olive trees and grape arbors, cultivated and harvested using techniques that may be older still. We drink the wine at dinner. I write in English but am surrounded by Italian, two modern languages with prehistoric roots in Indo-European. My writing is supported by the Rockefeller Foundation, a modern incarnation of an ancient tradition of philanthropy and patronage. I write on a laptop computer, the latest advance in the equally ancient tradition of scribes and scholars.

The traditions that surround me, then, are both ancient and living. The cultural knowledge that they represent—the tools for making sense of and living in the world—draw from the past but speak to the present and the future: the wine must age; my words will pass from my computer screen to a printed page, and perhaps to a database in an electronic library. So it is with all of the traditions that surround us—those of architecture, agriculture, engineering, the arts, religion, history, science, mathematics, literature. They are traditions of knowledge-in-action, deeply contextualized ways of participating in the world of the present. They live through their use, not through the passing on of knowledge-out-of-context.

Though we sit in the midst of many kinds of traditions, the ones on which I will focus are primarily linguistic. I will be concerned with the traditions of discourse within which we preserve and transform our cultural knowledge, and in particular with how students can better be taught to enter into those traditions through formal schooling.

Discussions of curriculum in American schools and colleges have usually focused on what is most worth knowing: Should we stress the Great Books, the richness of multiculturalism, the basic literacy needed in the worlds of work and leisure? But these arguments have been based on false premises and reflect a fundamental misconception of the nature of knowing. They strip knowledge of the contexts that give it meaning and vitality, and lead to an education that stresses knowledge-out-of-context rather than knowledge-in-action. In such a system, students are taught about the traditions of the past, and not how to enter into and participate in those of the present and future.

In this book, I offer a vision of curriculum that redresses that balance, placing the emphasis on the knowledge-in-action that is at the heart of all living traditions. Such knowledge arises out of participation in ongoing conversations about things that matter, conversations that are themselves embedded within larger traditions of discourse that we have come to value (science, the arts, history, literature, and mathematics, among many others). When we take this metaphor seriously, the development of curriculum becomes the development of culturally significant domains for conversation, and instruction becomes a matter of helping students learn to participate in conversations within those domains.

In elaborating my argument, I explore the ambiguities in my subtitle: Traditions can transform the individual, providing powerful tools for understanding experience; individuals also transform traditions, through the ways in which they make use of and move beyond the tools they inherit; and to ensure that this continues to occur, our traditions of teaching and learning must be transformed so that students learn to enter into the ongoing conversations that incorporate our past and shape our future.

. . . .

The Individual
and Tradition

If, as I will argue, curriculum needs to be rethought in order to foster students' entry into living traditions of knowledge-in-action rather than static traditions of knowledge-out-of-context, what is the nature of such traditions in individual and cultural life? What does it mean to enter into culturally significant traditions of knowing and doing? By examining the relationships between individuals and the traditions of knowing and doing amid which they live, this chapter provides a framework for thinking about what we should expect of our schools and colleges.

The social world of which any individual is a part is richly structured with traditions of knowing and doing that affect all aspects of life. Many of these traditions are encoded in cultural systems of symbolic representation—language, the arts, mathematics, science, religion, history. Each of these is a system of knowledge-in-action, a universe of cultural activity with characteristic ways of knowing and doing as well as characteristic content (on such traditions see Cassirer 1944; S. Langer 1942). For the individual, these systems of representation and the traditions encoded within them represent potential fields of activity, domains for entering into and taking part in culturally appropriate ways of knowing and doing. "Taking part" is key in the relationships between individuals and these larger cultural universes. We each must learn to take part in the traditions that encompass the knowledge of the larger culture, and remake them as our own.

THE TRADITIONS OF EVERYDAY LIFE

What does this process of entering into traditions look like? There is nothing particularly mysterious about it; in fact it is so natural that the most obvious examples are transparent, going on all the time without being noticed except by the linguists and psychologists and anthropologists whose business it is to study such things. The first sets of traditions in which we each learn to take part are those of the home and immediate family. These are traditions of language use, of roles and relationships, of individuality and communality that differ from family to family and community to community. These traditions form the background against which the more formal learning of the school will eventually take place.

There are many different genres of language use embedded in the traditions of everyday life. We learn ways to share information, to greet friends and say goodbye, to tell stories, to worship. Such genres are highly conventionalized; in learning to use them, the individual learns appropriate content and structure, as well as a web of expectations about when and how each genre may be used. As such they are a good example of knowledge-in-action: Though children learn at an early age how to use them, scholars still debate how to describe the knowledge that genres reflect (just as they debate how best to describe language itself).

The many forms of storytelling provide a good illustration of the different kinds of knowledge-in-action that learning the genres of everyday life may encompass. Though storytelling seems to occur universally across cultures, expectations about stories—what a story is, how it is to be interpreted, and when it may be appropriate to tell—may differ markedly from family to family and culture to culture. The traditions of storytelling that children learn first are those of their homes and families. In some families, storytelling is a context for demonstrating individual creativity and verbal play; in some, it is a context for accurate recital of events (and deviations are taken as lying); in some, it is a communal activity, with shared parts and multiple authorship (see Applebee 1978; Heath 1983; Blum-Kulka and Snow 1992; Wolf and Heath 1992). Thus the traditions of storytelling that are available for children to take part in, like other traditions of knowing, provide both a resource for the individual to exploit and a set of constraints on what will be appropriate to do.

In some cultures, stories provide a bridge from the oral culture of everyday life to literate traditions that are reinforced in formal schooling. Andrea Fishman has described (1990) the ways in which an Amish family encouraged even preschool children to take part in the literate world that played a central role in family as well as religious life. Recounting six-year-old Eli's preschool experiences with literacy, Fishman noted,

> Because oral reading as modeled by [Eli's father] is often imitated by the others, Eli, Jr., always shared his books by telling what he saw or knew about them. No one ever told him that telling isn't the same as reading, even though they may look alike, so Eli always seemed like a reader to others and felt like a reader himself. When everyone else sat reading or playing reading-involved games in the living room after supper or on Sunday afternoons, Eli did the same, to no one's surprise, to everyone's delight, and with universal, though often tacit, welcome and approval. When the other children received books as birthday and Christmas presents, Eli received them too. And when he realized at age six that both of his brothers had magazine subscriptions of their own, Eli asked for and got one as well. Eli never saw his own reading as anything other than real; he did not see it as make-believe or bogus, and neither did anyone else. (P. 32)

At first glance, Fishman's account seems an ideal representation of family support for literacy. But she goes on to emphasize that the ways in which even preschool children are involved in reading and writing embody certain assumptions about what taking part in these activities will mean. The literacy events of Eli's household emphasize accurate recall, the ability to discover the single right answer to every question, the ability to empathize with people in texts and perceive the moral lesson their experiences teach, and formulaic affirmations of a shared social world. They do not encourage speculation about possibilities or alternatives, analysis of motives, or enumeration of parts. Reading materials are limited to safe topics, distributed by the family's church or church-related organizations, or scanned for appropriateness by the adults in the household. And literacy learning will end at the eighth grade, as it did for Eli's parents. Other kinds of traditions of literacy—of creativity, for example, or of argument and analysis—would be viewed by Eli's Amish parents as a threat to the traditions that structure their home and community. (Indeed, when the teacher at the local school, herself Amish, introduces some changes in the curriculum, she is dismissed; see Fishman 1988.)

Thus even for a child as young as Eli, reading and writing are highly contextualized forms of knowledge-in-action, embedded in the traditions within which they are acquired. Being literate involves much more than just the ability to decode and encode written language; it involves ways of thinking—ways of literate thinking, as Judith Langer (1987) has called them—that shape the sense that will be made of text and of the world. In becoming literate within his world, Eli is taking on intellectual traditions—cultural tools—valued by his parents, his community, and his religion. They provide him with new ways of knowing and doing, of making sense of the world around him. Like all traditions, they open some possibilities and close off others; and as living traditions, they will continue to grow and change in response to new circumstances. (Thus the Amish, who may seem anachronistic to outsiders in modern American culture, have successfully adapted to the change around them. Eli, as he grows older, will become part of the continuing process of change and adaptation, working within or even against the culture he has become part of.)

THE TRADITIONS OF THE SCHOOL

The genres of everyday life are the genres acquired in the process of taking on the traditions of the home, family, and immediate communities in which the individual participates. There exist, however, many other genres that have evolved in more specialized traditions of knowing and doing—in the workplace, in schools, in the professions, and in academic disciplines. Like the genres of everyday life, these specialized genres offer the individual new ways of knowing and doing, of making sense of and sharing ideas and experiences.

Education in general (and formal schooling in particular) is fundamentally a process of mastering new traditions of discourse. These traditions begin with elaboration of the discourses of everyday life—storytelling, sharing of information, understanding the roles and relationships of home, school, and community. Such discourses become increasingly specialized and formal as a student moves through the educational system—evolving in most cases into the discourses characteristic of the academic disciplines. Each constitutes a set of cultural tools for analyzing experience within a particular domain of interest and identity—and situating oneself in relationship to it.

In acquiring these tools, students are learning to participate in a variety of socially constituted traditions of meaning-making that are valued in the cultures of which they are a part. These traditions include not just concepts and associated vocabulary, but also the rhetorical structures, the patterns of action, that are part of any tradition of meaning-making. They include characteristic ways of reaching consensus and expressing disagreement, of formulating arguments and providing evidence, as well as characteristic genres for organizing thought and conversational action. In mastering such traditions, students learn not only how to operate within them, but also how to change them.

The specialized genres with which I am most concerned here are those of the academic disciplines. There is nothing particularly sacred about the way the academic world is currently divided: Academic knowledge has been organized in a variety of ways at different times (from the trivium and the quadrivium to the highly differentiated specialties of the American research university), and fields of specialization have been organized, reorganized, subdivided, and combined on a relatively regular basis. The field of English studies is itself relatively recent in origin, though it builds upon fields of study (logic, rhetoric, oratory) that go back to the philosophers of ancient Greece and Rome. What the academic disciplines do represent at any given moment in time is the current state of an ongoing dialogue about significant aspects of human knowledge and experience. The disciplines exist because thoughtful people care about the traditions of knowing and doing that they represent; they are culturally significant in the sense that they are sustained by a culture over time and place, and in the sense that they are continued beyond the life of any particular individual. Any given tradition of knowing and doing may lose its significance as the dialogue among individuals, cultures, and traditions continues; thus such fields as alchemy and phrenology have lost their relevance and no longer sustain serious discourse. We study them today for what they may tell us about other times and places, rather than for direct insight into our own.

Such processes of change lead not only to the disappearance of some fields, but to the appearance or reorganization of others. Thus recent years have seen the emergence of cognitive science out of linguistics, psychology, and computer science. As fields reorganize, the conventions of conversation change with them.

Entry into the discourses of specialized fields usually takes place through formal schooling, although other routes are possible and, in some fields, typical. In the United States, elementary school students are usually at least introduced to the fields of science, mathematics, literature, history, civics, and geography; in the secondary school, students in an academic track are expected to engage in formal study of each of these fields, as well as a foreign language. At the college level, a similar pattern of general education in a variety of fields is usually ensured by distribution requirements that must be met before graduation. The rationale for such requirements has to do with achieving a ''well-rounded'' education. Implicitly, such requirements recognize that the various traditions of knowing and doing represented by these fields provide different tools for making sense of the world, tools that complement rather than substitute for one another.

We can begin to get a sense of what those tools are by looking at some recent discussions of what it means to "know" a field. Michael Polanyi, a chemist and philosopher, has pointed out (1958) that even the most objective or scientific ways of knowing are fundamentally personal—relying on what he calls the *tacit knowledge* of participants in the dialogue out of which the field is constituted. Tacit knowledge is the background against which all inquiry proceeds; it provides a matrix of taken-for-granted assumptions, rules of evidence and procedure, and a sense of what is interesting and what is less so. Tacit knowledge is knowledge-in-action; it grows out of involvement in the tradition rather than from articulating rules of procedure. In an oft-cited example, Polanyi contrasts the formal knowledge that describes how a bicycle stays upright with the tacit knowledge of the rider who is balanced on it:

> [The bicyclist] continues to keep . . . in balance
> by winding along a series of appropriate curvatures.
> A simple analysis shows that for a given angle of un-
> balance the curvature of each winding is inversely
> proportional to the square of the speed at which the
> cyclist is proceeding.
>
> But does this tell us exactly how to ride a bicycle?
> No. You obviously cannot adjust the curvature of
> your bicycle's path in proportion to the ratio of your
> unbalance over the square of your speed; and if you
> could you would fall off the machine, for there are a
> number of other factors to be taken into account in
> practice which are left out in the formulation of this
> rule. Rules of art can be useful, but they do not de-
> termine the practice of an art. (P. 50)

Just as the bicyclist must develop a tacit understanding of how to stay upright, novices who seek to participate in specialized traditions must learn the knowledge-in-action out of which the field is constituted. This knowledge will come from their participation in the tradition, their development of shared exemplars and shared experiences, rather than from study of knowledge-out-of-context or memorization of rules of procedure (see Kuhn 1962/1970; Latour 1987).

Recent studies in a variety of fields have made it clear how important the tacit knowledge that Polanyi describes is to all fields of endeavor. For my purposes here, I will review two traditions that seemingly have little in common—the representational arts and the hard sciences.

The Arts

Ernst Gombrich, in *Art and Illusion* (1968), has looked at length at the development of such features as perspective in pictorial and sculptural arts. Drawing examples from a wide range of cultures and periods, Gombrich argues that even the most talented and innovative artists approach their work through their preconceived notions of the characteristics of the figures they are re-creating. The artist "begins not with his visual impression but with his idea or concept" (p. 73), whether depicting a castle, a town, or the human form. This concept—or "schema," as Gombrich refers to it—is matched to the scene being depicted, and individual features of a particular castle, town, or person are imposed upon that preexisting concept. The concept suggests not only how a depiction will be rendered, but what is interesting to render at all.

From this beginning, Gombrich goes on to argue that the concept of a "language of art" is more than a loose metaphor; that in fact the artist draws on a set of ways of representation that, like language, are highly developed and conventionalized. Rather than being a direct depiction of what the artist sees, a painting is thus encoded in a language of tradition that provides the tools of representation without which art could not function:

> Even Dutch genre paintings that appear to mirror life
> in all its bustle and variety will turn out to be cre-
> ated from a limited number of types and gestures,
> much as the apparent realism of the picaresque

novel or of Restoration comedy still applies and mod-
ifies stock figures which can be traced back for centuries. There is no neutral naturalism. The artist, no
less than the writer, needs a vocabulary before he
can embark on a "copy" of reality. (P. 87)

The tools of representation, however, are not fixed and unchanging. They are learned by the artist, whose ways of seeing
are shaped by experiences with other paintings. And as with
other traditions, the tools of representation provide starting
points that are modified in a process of schema-matching and
correction, which later artists may choose to reject altogether.
Even a rejection, however, becomes a statement within the
tradition, a change that is recognized *as* change because of the
context of what has come before. Gombrich traces the evolution of naturalistic representation from its beginnings in primi-
tive cave drawing through the work of the Egyptians, Greeks,
and Romans to its high point in nineteenth-century painting,
and moves from there to the shift to nonrepresentational art
in the late nineteenth and early twentieth centuries. His basic
point remains the same, however: The artist does not duplicate
what he or she sees or feels, whether in inner or outer worlds.
Instead the artist renders within an acquired medium of expression and representation, "a medium grown up through
tradition and skill—that of the artist and that of the beholder"
(p. 370). Both artist and beholder can be part of the tradition
precisely because art operates within a structured style governed by technique and the conventions of tradition: It is these
that make an understanding audience possible, even as the
artist rejects or reformulates the basic conventions. The same
processes of shared understanding enable us to recognize the
stylized depictions on an Attic vase and the severity of a Mon-
drian painting, though the particular conventions that characterize each are completely different.

Gombrich contrasts his argument with traditional histories
of representation, which treat artistic development as the
closer approximation of natural "truth"—the discovery of
rules of perspective that allow more accurate depiction of "na-

ture" in its ideal form. On the contrary, Gombrich asserts, the history of representation is a history of a changing vocabulary of representation, of schemas that determine what is perceived as well as what is depicted. These changes are themselves part of a larger social context that exists within both the history of the field and the concerns of the day.

As Gombrich points out, the basic argument about the nature of progress and change has close parallels in the history of science, and it is to that field that I will now turn.

The Sciences

Thomas Kuhn, in *The Structure of Scientific Revolutions* (1962/1970), challenges the popular positivist conception of progress in the physical sciences as the gradual accumulation of knowledge and the closer approximation of objective truth. Examining key episodes from the history of science (including the work of Copernicus, Newton, Lavoisier, and Einstein), Kuhn argues that normal science depends on a shared set of unarticulated beliefs and procedures that he calls the *paradigms* underlying a field. Knowledge of these paradigms is tacit in Polanyi's sense. It is knowledge-in-action: Individuals learn the underlying paradigms in their field through their experiences with shared exemplars—significant problems, measurement instruments, laboratory technologies, and accepted solutions that show them how problems in the field may be solved. New scientists are in effect socialized into a community of shared practices and beliefs against which their work will be judged. Normal science in Kuhn's framework is essentially a puzzle-solving enterprise, involving the gradual extension of accepted principles to new problems. This activity looks very like the traditional concept of scientific progress as the gradual accumulation of new information. Kuhn argues, however, that major advances in science (such as those of Copernicus, Newton, Lavoisier, and Einstein) represent breaks in this accumulated wisdom. Rather than resulting from an accumulation of new information, scientific revolutions result from a fundamental shift in the underlying paradigm, leading scientists to interpret old observations in new ways, and to reconfigure what is considered relevant, interesting, or anomalous. The accumulated information that has resulted from previous scientific endeavor is reformulated: Some may now seem simply irrelevant or uninteresting, some will be reinterpreted in new but still interesting ways, and some will be rejected as inaccurate or mistaken. Kuhn provides some striking examples of how the most seemingly objective observations are conditioned by the tacit assumptions of the scientists carrying them out. As paradigms have changed, so have such seeming invariants as astronomical measurements and atomic weights. This is because the paradigms out of which scientists operate provide not just explanations of what they "observe," but frames of reference that help them "see" in the first place. When observations are ambiguous, scientists record data that conform to the expectations shaped by the paradigm within which they operate—at least until they notice enough anomalies to lead them to reformulate the paradigm itself.

Others have gone even further than Kuhn in unraveling the myths of objectivity and impersonal truth that surround the scientific endeavor. Paul Feyerabend, for example, has argued (1975) that because powerful new ideas in science are likely to look irrational against the background of established thought, science depends in important ways on irrationality. Similarly, Bruno Latour, examining the development of new ideas and new technologies, describes (1987) the highly social and political processes that characterize science in action, determining which discoveries are accepted, how they are developed, and how quickly they may be superseded. The images of scientific knowledge that emerge from such analyses are infinitely more complex, personal, and embedded in context than the image of scientific knowledge as the result of applying the scientific method to uncover nature's truths. Scientific knowledge as described by all of these commentators is thus knowledge-in-action, emerging out of and dependent for its meaning on the complexities of living traditions of scientific discourse.

PAST, PRESENT, FUTURE

Knowledge-in-action is positioned in an interesting way with respect to both the past and the present. A tradition (of ritual, of art, of inquiry, of behavior) as it exists at any point in time is oriented toward present activity: To participate in a tradition of discourse is to affirm (and also to define) its present relevance. By participating we affirm its relevance; by the way we participate, we define the way it is relevant—what is presently interesting or significant.

Knowledge-in-action is also an interpretation of the past. It represents a synthesis of what we choose to remember and how we choose to remember it. As our present concerns change and develop, history is reconstructed to reflect our current understanding. Thus the past is always a living part of the present, and in a very real sense dependent on it. We have seen this process at work in Kuhn's scientific revolutions and their aftermath: The most objective of measurements are redefined, and earlier findings are reconstrued in both their detail and their relationships to one another. In this way, as Wendell Harris notes (1994) in discussing the notion of literary history, the way we interpret the past is directly dependent on the argument we want to make about the present:

> The changes chronicled . . . are almost necessarily
> assumed to be identified in part with the character of
> the nation or people. . . . The narrative constructed
> is assumed not only to cast light on the historical de-
> velopment of the literature, but to use the literature
> to illustrate the present happy or sad state of the cul-
> ture. (P. 445)

As the present changes, the past will of necessity be reconstrued—a process that Kuhn also notes in the continual rewriting of the past to reflect the present in science textbooks. Thus history must always be as much an interpretation of the present as it is a reconstrual of the past.

As this discussion implies, traditions of discourse are not static; knowledge-in-action shapes our expectations about the future as well as our interpretations of the past. Those expectations can be changed, as we act within or against the traditions of which we are a part. During the past few decades, for example, a vigorous feminist tradition has developed in many fields, inviting participants to reconstruct or abandon previous traditions of knowing and doing that ignore or devalue the contributions of women (Fetterley 1978; Minnich 1990). In literature, readers are encouraged to read against traditional texts, to resist the "willing suspension of disbelief" in order to uncover underlying stereotypes, prejudices, and male-dominated systems of values. Such arguments can have profound effects on future actions: In literature, for example, feminist criticism has led to the reevaluation of many canonical texts, the rehabilitation of many noncanonical authors, and the discovery and incorporation into the larger literary tradition of a history of women's writing that was previously ignored. The point for the moment, however, is that even as feminist critics argue against the tradition, they are working within it, relying on their knowledge-in-action to make their arguments about what is objectionable or misguided, or simply missing. When Deanne Bogdan (1990) critiques John Updike's often-anthologized short story "A&P," for example, her readings depend on her knowledge of expected, conventionalized reactions to the characters and actions, and it is on these "traditional" readings that she and her students focus when they offer a new set of approaches to the text.

The traditions of knowledge-in-action in which we participate do not simply constrain us, but are open to analysis and change. Indeed, traditions remain vital only to the extent that they continue to address the present and the future as well as the past, providing satisfactory frameworks for addressing issues that concern us. Harold Bloom has written (1973) about the "anxiety" caused by the influence of the past—the poet's need to reject the traditions from which he or she springs in order to claim originality and creativity. Every poet believes that

> a poet's stance, his Word, his imaginative identity, his whole being, *must* be unique to him, and remain

unique, or he will perish, as a poet, if ever even he has
managed his re-birth into poetic incarnation. But this
fundamental stance is as much also his precursor's as
any man's fundamental nature is also his father's, however transformed, however turned about. (P. 71)

Though the individual poet, like any radical critic of contemporary traditions, may deny the process, this transformation and
turning about of the past is exactly the pattern of imitation, limitation, and rebirth that one would expect as part of any vital,
living tradition—similar in fact to Kuhn's pattern of paradigm
and revolution. As Bloom points out, even the greatest poets,
whom we most honor for their originality and uniqueness, are
deeply part of the traditions of the past. "Every poet is a being
caught up in a dialectical relationship (transference, repetition,
error, communication) with another poet or poets" (p. 91).

The process of reconstrual of the tradition is very evident
in the history of literary studies, as my reference to the work
of feminist critics has already suggested. The treatment of
Shakespeare can provide a specific example. As Lawrence
Levine has reminded us (1988), in the early nineteenth century, Shakespeare was a part of American popular culture.
Plays were performed in taverns and meeting halls, and bur-
lesqued on the music-hall stage. Differing styles of presentation were a matter of public debate—and could provoke the
kind of public conflict and even riots that today are more associated with athletic rivalries. By the end of the century, however, the Shakespearean tradition had been transformed into
an academic tradition; the focus of debate had shifted from
performance and style to the arcane details of variorum editions. Great scholars ensured that Shakespeare became difficult—a matter for the academy and for an academic elite.

Even within the academy the tradition of Shakespearean
criticism has been anything but unchanging. Debates about
variorum editions were followed by explorations of Elizabe-
than culture, and these in turn by New Critical analyses of the
form and balance of the plays outside of their historical contexts. In more recent decades, the tools of deconstruction,

feminism, Marxist criticism, and ethnic studies have been brought to bear, each providing a different perspective on the accomplishments (and shortcomings) of the Shakespearean canon. Changes in Shakespearean criticism have been unusual only in that Shakespeare has continued to be a major focus of attention even as traditions of scholarship have evolved; the fate of others has been less certain, with cycles of rejection and rehabilitation depending on the relevance of particular authors and periods to contemporary critical concerns. Thus for example interest in John Donne and the metaphysical poets was rekindled because of the New Critics' interest in structure and symbol, while a whole range of women and authors of color have been reconstructed in the postmodern era.

PERSONAL KNOWLEDGE
AND PUBLIC KNOWLEDGE

From storytelling to Shakespearean criticism, traditions of knowing and doing can be very rich and very complicated. How then does the individual learn to participate without being overwhelmed by all that there is to learn? When individuals enter into new traditions of knowledge-in-action, they take on new ways of making sense of the world and of experience. Children like Eli learn traditions of discourse because they are enabled to do things in the world of their present, and they learn them through their actions and the help that others provide. In a very real sense, Eli learns to read *by* reading, in the company of his parents, siblings, and schoolmates. He learns to do what a reader does—talking about books, asking and answering appropriate questions, learning the relationships between words and symbols, participating with others in the world of stories until, eventually, he is able to participate on his own.

Just as children's learning of the genres of everyday life represents an active participation in a tradition, entry into the traditions of discourse represented by the academic disciplines requires an active reconstruction of the disciplinary matrix. This reconstruction may take place at a great distance from the "cutting edge" of the discipline, yet for the individual it represents new mastery of new ways of making sense—it extends understanding, and the possibility of order and control, of the world within which we live. The issues being discussed in a particular elementary classroom may be at some remove from those being discussed in graduate seminars, but the discussions are nonetheless part of an exploration of the same culturally significant domain for conversation. As Carl Bereiter has pointed out (1994) in talking about science education, even at the cutting edges of a field the many individual discussions that are carried on do not move at the same pace or even necessarily in the same direction. There is no reason to treat them as different in kind from the discussions that take place in school or college classrooms.

LIVING TRADITIONS

The point that I have been making can be put simply: The kinds of learning that matter for our schools and colleges represent traditions of knowledge-in-action. These traditions are dynamic and changing, acquired through participation, and oriented toward present and future rather than past. In learning to participate in these traditions, an individual is taking on a dynamic set of tools for being in and making sense of the world. Any conception of education that strips these tools of their contexts, or focuses on their past rather than their present relevance and future potential, will be debilitating for the individual and for society as well.

But, as will become clear in chapter 3, the curriculum as it is presently organized leads to just this sort of debilitation, focusing primarily on knowledge-out-of-context. Proponents on the left and right—of multiculturalism and social justice as well as of Great Books and traditional values—cast their proposals in terms of what students should learn *about,* and in the process they strip knowledge of its most vital contexts. Moving away from this emphasis toward a curriculum organized around knowledge-in-action—a curriculum that might even invite students to participate in the debates that are currently ongoing—will require new ways of thinking about what we teach and why.

Deadly Traditions

In this chapter I will take a close look at the traditions of education that have shaped American schools and colleges. I will argue that these traditions have engendered an emphasis on knowledge-out-of-context rather than knowledge-in-action, even though the rhetoric of education has long stressed such goals as the development of a well-rounded intellect. That early commentators sought to achieve these goals through the study of Latin and Greek, and later commentators in studies in various disciplines taught in English, has made little difference. Progressives and conservatives alike have argued that students should be taught to arrive at new understandings, to think for themselves, to become independent knowers and doers. This in turn will produce flexible lifelong learners able to adapt to changing conditions in the workplace, the home, and the global community. Few teachers in any subject area would argue with these goals, and virtually every academic discipline, from the arts (Eisner 1982) to mathematics (Anderson et al. 1994), has sought to position itself within such a framework.

But these goals are rarely attained. Commentators in subjects as diverse as science, math, history, and English (Bereiter 1994; Anderson et al. 1994; Wineburg 1991; Seixas 1993; Brown 1991) have lamented the extent to which learning becomes a matter of memorization and recitation, where the teacher is seen as the provider of knowledge that the student is expected to replicate. Students, too, note the discrepancy between grand goals of exploration and discovery, and the ways in which classroom interaction unfolds. As an example of their perceptions, let me use Brett, a student typical of many who have participated in my studies of literature instruction (Applebee 1993b, 1994). Asked to comment on a particular senior high school Contemporary Literature course, he quickly moves on to his experiences with teachers in general:

> She wanted us to figure it out so she asked us questions about it. I didn't really enjoy it that much, because it seems like most of the teachers know the answer they are looking for and then they will sort of hint up to that answer and they won't be satisfied until they get that answer, even though they are trying to make us think for ourselves. It is odd like that. . . . I don't think it would really bother me if their objectives were to teach us like that, but they say their objective is to make us think for ourselves, but if they wanted to take the attitude that "now I'm to explain this to you how the author intended you to feel," it wouldn't be so bad.

"It is odd like that," says Brett, and his reactions are all too typical of those of students across the generations. James B. Angell, describing expectations at Brown University in 1845, put it this way:

> There was a general belief among the students, though no formal statement to that effect was made by the Faculty, that they would gain higher credits by repeating the language of the book than by reporting the substance of the thought in their own language. (Cited in Graff 1987, p. 32)

To begin to understand what has been happening, I want to look explicitly at the teaching of literature, though the experiences there are typical of those in other subjects.

LITERATURE IN SCHOOL AND COLLEGE

The English curriculum as we know it came into being in the late nineteenth century, when a variety of separate studies (reading, literary history, composition, grammar, spelling, and oratory, among others) were collected together as a new subject, English. (On the early history of English as a school subject, see Applebee 1974; on English in colleges, see Graff 1987 and Russell 1991.) Within this amalgam, literature was justified largely as a reservoir of cultural values and a source of moral strength. This tradition was given fullest expression in the works of Matthew Arnold (1867), who treated the arts in general and literature in particular as embodying the cultural knowledge of the great Western tradition, winnowed by time and sanctioned by genius. Writing in reaction to the disruptions being caused by the industrial revolution, Arnold saw in such culture a new principle of authority that could replace the eroding bonds of class and religion. The alternative, he warned, was anarchy.

In spite of the high moral justifications for literary study, the early history of the teaching of literature is not a particularly happy one. Literature entered the curriculum at a time when education focused on training and exercising the mental faculties, in particular the faculties of "memory" and "reason." (These twin emphases foreshadow a concern with what, in the previous chapter, I have called knowledge-in-action, involving both knowing *and* doing, though early commentators lacked an awareness of the importance of tacit knowledge in such processes.) The problem for literary studies in the nineteenth century was that they seemed to lack both a content to memorize and a method of study to exercise the faculty of reason. Without a rigorous methodology of its own, literature borrowed instead from related traditions in rhetoric, literary history, and philology, or remained outside the curriculum as something to be enjoyed but not subject to academic study. (Literary societies flourished in both school and college, and often had better libraries than the schools or colleges they were associated with.)

Rhetorical studies of English literature date to the middle of the eighteenth century, when a group of Scottish rhetoricians began to analyze the rhetorical features of classical (Latin and Greek) as well as vernacular (French and English) texts. The approach was prescriptive, using the classical texts to derive and illustrate rules of diction, style, and the uses of figurative language. Out of this tradition came courses in "rhetoric," "analysis," and "criticism," in which a literary text would be critically examined to ensure that it conformed to the prescriptive rules of grammar and rhetoric, all in the ultimate service of the students' speaking and writing skills. The rhetoric handbooks that promoted such studies included their own examples and did not require that any literature be read at all, but by the middle of the nineteenth century some schools and colleges were also using individual works of literature for parsing and analysis.

At about the same time, literary history also emerged as an important aspect of English studies. This took as its model the studies of ancient civilizations that were a well-established part of the classical curriculum. Though both the classical curriculum and its English translation began with broad and humanistic goals, an emphasis on rote facts and memorization quickly dominated virtually all applications. Charles Cleveland's history of English literature (1849), which became a popular text for both school and college, contained encyclopedic information about each author, including dates, titles, and immediate and historical reactions. Although excerpts were also provided, the accompanying "Questions for Examination" reflect the emphases that mattered: Of Lady Russell they ask, "Whose wife? . . . What does Burnett say of her letters?" Of Milton, "What is his first poetical work, and what its subject? What the second? Third? Fourth? Fifth? Sixth? Seventh? Eighth? Ninth? Tenth? . . . What does Brydges say of Johnson's Life of Milton?" Such studies of knowledge-out-of-context remain an element of literature instruction to the present day.

The third early methodology for approaching literature was based on philology. Like rhetoric and literary history, philology also has its roots in classical studies, transposed by the German Romantics to the study of German and later of English. It began with the ideal of discovering and re-creating the cultural history of a nation, but (like literary history) was quickly overcome by pedantry. In 1867, for example, James Rolfe, a principal of Cambridge (Massachusetts) High School who had trained in philological studies at Harvard, prepared an American edition of *Julius Caesar*. His text included an introduction, a history of the play, the sources of the plot, critical comments on the play (26 pages), the play itself (102 pages), notes (82 pages), and an index of words and phrases explained (Mersand 1960, pp. 279–80). By the late 1800s, as Gerald Graff (1987) notes, philology even in the colleges had lost its connections to the broad humanistic tradition from which it had begun, and had become a separate study of language. Invoking the older, broader meaning of philology became only "a ceremonial gesture," or a "way of warding off criticism by depicting literary studies as they were supposed to be, rather than as they were" (p. 80).

The pattern of emphasis on memorization and rote learning—on knowledge-out-of-context—that developed in the early teaching of literature had its parallels throughout the school and college curriculum. And like the emphases that developed in the teaching of literature, these came about from the best of intentions. The early history of laboratory work in science instruction is a good example. This was introduced into the curriculum as part of an effort to legitimize the methods, conventions, and assumptions of the then-new research disciplines. Through laboratory work, students would be invited into the methods and procedures of the sciences. Laboratory work was quickly transformed in practice, however, from sites for research into a means to assess whether students had learned the right things. Colleges even began to require lab notebooks for college entrance, based on standard experiments that all students were expected to perform. To prevent "cheating," lab notebooks were locked up between laboratory sessions, further separating them from the disciplinary learning they were meant to foster. In the process, as David Russell has pointed out (1991), the laboratory work and the writing that went with it "came to be used as a means of exclusion, a means of setting and enforcing disciplinary standards, rather than as a means of introducing students to the scientific community through meaningful participation in its activity" (p. 95).

These early emphases set a pattern that has been repeated ever since. On the one hand, educators have offered goals that stress familiarity with and participation in the great cultural traditions that constitute the various academic disciplines—in terms of the faculty psychology of the nineteenth century, goals that emphasized both memory and reason. On the other hand, educators have relied on classroom practices that focus almost exclusively on memory, allowing goals of active reasoning and participation to fall by the wayside. Instead of the knowledge-in-action that both allows and develops through participation in culturally significant traditions of discourse, we have emphasized the knowledge-out-of-context that comes from studying its characteristics.

Just as the colleges specified a particular set of experiments as the basis of lab notebooks (and placed more emphasis on particular expected outcomes than on accurate but perhaps idiosyncratic observation), they also defined a literature curriculum that has had a very particular set of characteristics. Harvard established an English department in 1872 and quickly specified a list of specific titles as the basis for a new entrance requirement in English composition (for 1873–1874). The practice spread rapidly, and the authors and titles that formed the high school curriculum were soon determined in large part by college entrance requirements. In the first ten years (1874–1883), the requirements listed by American colleges included books by fifteen authors, listed here in order of their first appearance on the lists: Shakespeare (fourteen different titles), Goldsmith (three), Scott (ten), Irving (two), Byron (one), Thackeray (one), Macaulay (two), Addison (one), Gray (one), Johnson (one), Dickens (one), Carlyle (two), Milton (one), Hawthorne (one), and Eliot (two). This list of required authors, like the syllabus it constituted, was largely white, male, and Eurocentric—features that themselves would attract later criticism. But above all the list was authoritative, implying a body of knowledge, a universe of things to know that gave the new subject of English a place and a legitimacy within the curriculum as a whole. (Recall Rolfe's 1867 edition of *Julius Caesar,* a prototype for those that would later be published specifically for students preparing for these exams: Considerably less than half of the book was devoted to the play itself.)

Once in place, this curriculum remained remarkably stable, in spite of wave after wave of educational reform. Neither broad changes in educational philosophy nor narrower changes in literary criticism seriously displaced either the texts chosen for study or the emphasis on knowledge-out-of-context at the expense of knowledge-in-action. The remarkable stability since the 1890s is evident in two series of studies roughly fifty years apart: Dora V. Smith's analyses of the teaching of English in the 1930s and 1940s, and my own recent analyses of literature instruction in schools across the country (Applebee 1993b).

Smith's first study (1932), carried out as part of a federally sponsored National Survey of Secondary Education, was based on analyses of courses of study and visits to selected schools that presented unique features. At the senior high school level, she found that the curriculum in 50 percent of schools across the nation consisted simply of lists of classic texts for study. Comparing her results with an earlier survey of texts taught before 1900, Smith found that of the thirty most frequently taught texts, only Webster's *Bunker Hill Oration* had disappeared from the lists. Smith also found that as many as nine weeks were devoted to a single text in some classes. A few years later (1941), in a study that was limited to schools in New York State but that relied more on examination of student performance and classroom observations, Smith noted that students were in general more familiar with traditional literature than with books "of the present century" (p. 250). She also described the typical approach to such selections: "Question and answer procedures with the teacher in command, and recitation around the room of sentences written out at home the night before represent by far the most common activities of the average high school English class" (p. 253).

Nine weeks of such teaching were undoubtedly more than enough to kill interest in any book.

My own recent studies of the high school English curriculum highlight the extent to which the teaching of English remains defined by this tradition (Applebee 1992, 1993b). When I asked department chairs in schools across the country to list required book-length texts, the ten most frequently cited titles included *Romeo and Juliet, Macbeth, Huckleberry Finn, Julius Caesar, To Kill a Mockingbird, The Scarlet Letter, Of Mice and Men, Hamlet, The Great Gatsby,* and *Lord of the Flies.* Changes in individual selections were obvious, with (as in Smith's earlier study) the addition of some contemporary selections and some changes in the particular selections from favored authors (e.g., *Romeo and Juliet* vs. *Julius Caesar*). But with only a few exceptions, the hundreds of selections on the list as a whole remained white (98 percent), male (81 percent), and Eurocentric (99 percent), firmly in the tradition established before the turn of the century.

Although analyses of the college curriculum have been less detailed, surveys carried out by the Modern Language Association show a similar stability over time (Harris 1988; Huber and Laurence 1989; Huber 1992; Waller 1986). In spite of lively debates and dramatic changes in the paradigms governing graduate study in English in the past several decades, the undergraduate program has remained quite traditional both in the texts that are required and in the ways those texts are studied. (History of ideas and New Criticism lead the list of approaches cited as influential by instructors, even in upper division courses; feminist criticism ranks third [Huber 1992].) Most departments have responded to new movements in the field by adding additional courses—in feminist studies and African-American literature, for example—that students are not required to take. Hence the experience of most students (including those who will go on to teach in elementary and secondary schools) has remained relatively unchanged.

My studies also revealed a continuing emphasis on learning *about,* rather than participating *in,* traditions of literature and criticism (Applebee 1993b). In Nystrand and Gamoran's terms (1991, 1992), most classrooms emphasized recitation rather than "authentic" questions that encourage dialogue and debate. Although teachers claimed to have broad humanistic goals for literature instruction (building interest in reading, encouraging creativity and independent thinking), observation of classroom practice found that the teaching of literature continued to be a relatively traditional enterprise. Knowledge about text—in particular, knowledge of its parts and how they contribute to an agreed-upon "author's meaning"—dominated most lessons. Like Brett, most students were expected to figure out the answers that the teacher was looking for. (On the tensions between teachers' ideals and their classroom practices, see Marshall, Smagorinsky, and Smith 1995.) Opportunities to discuss alternative interpretations or students' own responses were relatively few. Widely used instructional materials reinforce these tendencies. In the literature anthologies that were most popular in the schools I studied, for example, the accompanying suggestions for writing and discussion activities were dominated by questions that focused on details of plot and vocabulary that were assumed to have one right answer (e.g., "When did Michelle decide to leave for town?" "What does 'verdant' in line 7 mean?"). All but a small proportion of the suggested activities emphasized the development of knowledge-out-of-context rather than knowledge-in-action.

In a related series of studies, my colleague Alan Purves examined the treatment of literature in formal assessments of what students are learning (1992). His samples ranged from the unit tests accompanying instructional materials at the middle and high school level to the standardized tests that colleges use for admissions and placement. He found that the questions that are posed about literature differ hardly at all from those that might be asked of expository prose (Brody, DeMilo, and Purves 1989). He also found that these questions are overwhelmingly likely to be posed in multiple-choice rather than open-ended formats, and to stress the same kinds of knowledge-out-of-context that I found in my studies of emphases in instruction. Louise Rosenblatt captured the spirit of these materials when she lamented (1978) that the workbook questions in a third-grade basal series asked, "What facts does this poem teach us?" (p. 39). Purves's favorite, offered in the same spirit, was a true-or-false question: "Huckleberry Finn was a good boy" (p. 20). If we think of literature as Rosenblatt once described it, as quiet conversation about good books (an image that honors the importance of knowledge-in-action), what we have instead is a kind of Trivial Pursuit—and one in which what should count as a right answer is not always obvious (*was* Huckleberry Finn a good boy?). Instead of a vital tradition of knowing and doing, we are left with fragments that make little sense to anyone involved.

CHANGING NOTIONS OF CURRICULUM

To a large extent the continuing emphasis on knowledge-out-of-context can be traced to the frameworks that we use to think about curriculum. As we have seen, vital traditions of discourse are grounded in tacit conventions that govern what is said, by whom, and in what ways. Particular traditions carry with them their own specialized content, reflected in a technical vocabulary and its associated concepts as well as in the rules of use governing discourse. That is, knowledge of a tradition involves both knowing and doing. Conceptions of curriculum, on the other hand, have focused only on the specialized content (the knowing), ignoring the discourse conventions that govern participation (the doing). Thus rather than learning to participate in the discourse—to construct and defend their own conclusions based on arguments and evidence appropriate to the traditions of literature, science, or history—students learn about its characteristics.

Curriculum development reinforces this emphasis on characteristics of, rather than participation in, a tradition of discourse. The typical approach to curriculum requires first a thorough parsing of what students should know, and second the organization of those parts into elaborate scope and sequence charts that specify the order in which that content should be taught. This technology for building curricula was developed in the early part of this century by such theorists as Franklin Bobbitt (1918; 1924), and was elaborated by several generations of scholars and teachers who were committed to task analysis and to a belief in the orderly development of subskills, the accumulation of the necessary building blocks of knowledge and skill. The technology that resulted was admirably appropriate for the development of knowledge-out-of-context.

Bobbitt, a professor of educational administration at the University of Chicago, dedicated himself to the development of a scientific approach to curriculum. He had little use for the broad platitudes that educators often use to justify their work, dismissing such goals as "culture," "moral character building," and "harmonious development of the individual" as at best "vague guesses" at objectives (1918, p. 41). Instead, he argued that human life, "however varied, consists in the performance of specific activities" (p. 42) that can be revealed through scientific study of behavior; the resulting lists of activities would yield specific objectives for the curriculum, objectives that would be "numerous, definite, and particularized." He began his own list of General Educational Objectives promisingly enough, with "1. Ability to use language in all ways required for proper and effective participation in the community life" (1924, p. 11). His comprehensiveness and particularity soon overwhelmed any special emphasis on language activities, however, and the list continued on to such objectives (in a final section on Unspecialized Practical Activities) as "813. Ability to perform the various activities involved in traveling and outdoor life" and "814. Ability to wisely select garments" (p. 29).

Bobbitt considered this listing "general," no more than an initial overview that would guide a more detailed enumeration of specific objectives in each curriculum area and at each grade level. Specialists in the various subject areas quickly took up the challenge. The National Council of Teachers of English, for example, set up a special committee to enumerate the various skills involved in the "ability to use language in all ways required" through a survey of as wide a variety of people as possible. (Some 22,000 questionnaires were distributed, but only 2,615 usable responses were obtained, a point that did not seem to bother the committee very much.) The survey led to specific recommendations about the skills that should receive more attention in the English curriculum:

> The schools might well devote more attention to a number of the language activities which according to the returns are widely used by persons of the many callings and social groups reporting, and which are reported as giving much difficulty. These activities in particular are: Interviewing: word of mouth inquiries; reports to a superior; instructions for subordinates; conferences. Conversation: with casual acquaintances; at social gatherings; over the telephone. Public Speaking: informal discussion; preparing addresses. Writing: informal notes and memos for one's self; formal notes of invitation, introduction, etc. Reading: legal documents. Listening: to an interview, a conference, or a public meeting. (Clapp 1926, p. 46)

Such a statement of desirable goals for the teaching of English is in form little different from the lists of individual selections for study that resulted from the earlier college entrance requirements. Such lists ensure coverage of desirable content or skills, but strip away the traditions of knowing and doing that give meaning and purpose to them. Firmly established in English and other subjects during the first part of the century, such lists of curriculum content became part of the larger model of diagnostic teaching and testing that was elaborated in the years that followed. Positivist in origin, this technology was oriented toward the teaching of information, of knowledge about the traditions of knowing that defined the curriculum. Such an approach is perfectly appropriate to a curriculum that construes knowledge as fixed and transmittable—as something "out there" to be memorized by students. It is appropriate to a curriculum of the names and dates in literary history or of rules of grammar and rhetoric, of phonics and vocabulary practice. Such a curriculum of knowledge-out-of-context may enable students to do well on multiple-choice items. It does not enable them to enter on their own into our vital academic traditions of knowing and doing. They lack the skills to develop a new interpretation, to analyze a new situation, or to muster evidence in support of new arguments and unexpected opinions. These are skills of knowledge-in-action, generated through participation in real dialogue, whether that dialogue focuses on formulating and defending one's own response to characters and situations or on applying an external frame of reference in order to articulate, for example, a feminist critique or a Freudian interpretation.

An emphasis on knowledge-out-of-context also leads many students to turn away from the traditions of knowing to which they are being introduced. To return to Polanyi's example in the previous chapter, they are forced to memorize the rules but are never allowed to ride the bicycle—and if they try on their own they are likely to fall off. For most students, such an experience is unpleasant. They begin school with considerable interest and enthusiasm, but they grow increasingly disillusioned with all subjects as they progress through school. Even reading and writing for their own purposes (rather than for school) becomes less attractive the longer students are in school. (The National Assessment of Educational Progress has tracked such declines across the grades since the early 1970s, when the assessments began. See for example Applebee et al. 1994; Langer et al. 1990.) Like Brett and the early students at Brown University whose comments were introduced at the beginning of this chapter, most students quickly understand that the game of school is to figure out the answer the teacher wants; and it is a game that many students simply do not want to play. Rather than stimulating and broadening the mind, the traditions of knowing introduced in the typical classroom are as deadly as that suggested by a playground rhyme that was popular when I was a high school student in upstate New York:

> Latin is a dead language,
> As dead as dead can be.
> First it killed the Romans,
> And now it's killing me.

It is less than comforting to realize that the protest this embodies stretches across the Atlantic and through the ages. Iona and Peter Opie gathered an almost identical verse from schoolchildren in Croydon, England (1959, p. 173), and cite similar complaints dating back to the sixteenth century.

Curriculum as Conversation

In previous chapters, I have explored the significant role that various traditions of discourse play in social and individual life. I have also examined how education has twisted those traditions, turning them from powerful forms of knowledge-in-action into powerless systems of knowledge-out-of-context. The problem for the present chapter is to consider how traditions might be construed more constructively in the context of schooling.

My starting point is to recognize that classroom discourse plays a critical mediating role between broader traditions and schooled knowledge. Classroom discourse in its various forms constitutes the traditions students will come to know. If students are to learn to enter into culturally significant schooled traditions of knowing and doing, they will do so through their participation in the language and culture of the classroom. A variety of recent studies have detailed the large differences in the cultures of knowledge-in-action that are established in the classrooms of different teachers. In ways large and small, teachers from preschool and primary (McGill-Franzen and Lanford 1994; Martinez and Teale 1993) to college and graduate school (Berkenkotter, Huckin, and Ackerman 1988; Herrington 1985; McCarthy 1987) establish not only the roles of teacher and learner, but also what will count as knowing in their classrooms. Thus as simple an activity as listening to a story read by the teacher will in one classroom require comments on characters and their actions, and in another, silence and an attentive demeanor. At the other end of the educational spectrum, something as specialized as participation in a graduate school course in chemical engineering will in one context be cooperative and creative, and in another require memorization and rehearsal of preestablished routines. "Learning to do school" (Dyson 1984) is thus always a highly situated activity occurring at the intersection of systems of social roles and expectations, previous experiences, and newer traditions of knowing and doing.

In learning to do school, students are in fact learning to enter into culturally significant traditions of knowing and doing. As we saw in chapter 2, in acting within these traditions, they are keeping company with the philosopher articulating a theory of knowing (Polanyi 1958), the artist painting within or against a tradition (Gombrich 1968), and the scientist revolutionizing a scientific discipline (Kuhn 1962/1970). All of these enterprises are characteristically social in nature: The words that are used, what counts as knowing and doing, are shaped by what other individuals have said and done, by the conversations that have gone before. This is the irreducible nature of tradition, which constitutes the present matrix out of which we act.

The problem for curriculum and instruction is to ensure that those traditions are constituted as systems of knowledge-in-action, available as tools to guide present and future behavior, rather than systems of knowledge-out-of-context, stripped of their constructive and constitutive potential. That means, in turn, that the process of schooling must be a process of actually entering into particular traditions of knowing and doing. Students must discuss literature they have read, not simply be taught about its characteristics; they must do science, not simply be told its results; and they must engage in mathematically based problem solving, not simply memorize formulas.

Such exhortations are not unfamiliar, nor have they been particularly effective in previous attempts to reconfigure the process of education (Cuban 1984; Tyack and Tobin 1994). For the most part, they have foundered from lack of rigor and lack of efficiency. If students are to learn by doing, how do schools avoid allowing them to wallow in their own ignorance? If they are to learn through discovery, how can schools avoid a long recapitulation of previous discoveries, most of which are no longer interesting or relevant? Such criticisms, far from missing the point, have often been well-justified. Progressive theories have relied more on the enthusiasm of gifted teachers than on well-articulated procedures of curriculum and instruction. Lively vignettes have replaced serious attempts at consensus about the structure and content of schooling (e.g., Lloyd-Jones and Lunsford 1989; International Reading Association and the National Council of Teachers of English 1989). Competing theories of education, on the other hand, have offered elaborate and well-structured alternatives that seem to guarantee an orderly and efficient process of education. Whether descended from Bobbitt and the analysis of life needs or based on armchair analyses of what is worth knowing (e.g. Hirsch 1987), these alternatives, as I argued in the previous chapter, generate curricula that, while orderly, are also quite deadly, creating systems of education that emphasize knowledge-out-of-context. If we are to reject them, however, the onus is upon us to provide an equally well-articulated structure to guide a more constructive system of education stressing knowledge-in-action.

A New Framework for Thinking about Curriculum

The recognition that classroom discourse mediates between broader cultural traditions and schooled knowledge leads to a new way to think about curriculum and instruction: A curriculum provides domains for conversation, and the conversations that take place within those domains are the primary means of teaching and learning. Through such conversations, students will be helped to enter into culturally significant traditions of knowledge-in-action. In most schools, these traditions will reflect major academic disciplines—language, history, literature, science, the arts—though they can just as easily be interdisciplinary or cross-disciplinary, or be based on the traditions of the home, community, or workplace.

Curriculum involves a selection out of such living traditions of discourse, a point that I try to capture through the emphasis on *domains* for conversation. Domains are selections of topics or issues out of a larger tradition, and as a set are overlapping and multiple rather than taxonomic. They will be larger or smaller in scope depending on the level at which curriculum is being discussed. That is, we can talk about the domains for conversation in a single segment of a course in the college curriculum, or about the domains for conversation that constitute a college major in a specific field. The scope of the former domains will be much more precise and limited, those of the latter broader and more generalized.

Rather than providing sharp boundaries of inclusion and exclusion, domains define the saliency of different experiences to the overall conversation: some are more central, others less so, and there is usually a wide range in between. The domain for a conversation in a college course on Anglo-Saxon literature, for example, is likely to treat *Beowulf* as central, but there are a variety of other texts that might be more or less central depending on the conversation that was envisioned. *The Odyssey* might become part of the domain if the conversation were extended to include an exploration of the characteristics of early epics; Milton or Shakespeare might appear if the conversation turned to the Anglo-Saxon legacy in later literature. In any particular curriculum, certain parts of the conversational domain are likely to be determined in advance by the teacher or the department, and other parts to evolve as the conversation progresses.

A conversational domain can include many different kinds of experiences for students to share, and many different voices, including those of the past as well as the present. The particular voices and experiences that are included will be determined by many different factors, including the maturity and previous experience of the students and the demands of the local community. (The curricular conversation is unlikely to deal seriously with relativity theory in the first grade, nor is it likely in public schools in the United States to deal with biblical exegesis.)

Exploring a conversational domain—making sense of the experiences and voices—also involves engaging in particular ways of thinking and doing that are associated with the domain (and with the larger tradition of discourse of which it is a part). Exploring a topic in science, for example, involves using different rules of argument and evidence than will be used in mathematics, and both will differ from history. It is these ways of knowing, thinking, and doing, this knowledge-in-action, that students will acquire as they are helped to enter into significant traditions of discourse. They provide new tools to explore and make sense of the world. And as we gain control over these tools and the discourses in which they are embedded, we learn, as the linguist Michael Halliday has put it (1977), how to mean.

The notion that education provides students with entry into ongoing cultural conversations about their lives and the world in which they live is usually cited in passing rather than being taken seriously as a starting point for thinking about issues of curriculum. Graff (1992) captures its essence nicely when he comments:

> In short, reading books with comprehension, making arguments, writing papers, and making comments in a class discussion are *social* activities. They involve entering into a cultural or disciplinary conversation, a process not unlike initiation into a social club. (P. 77)

Taken seriously, the notion of a cultural or disciplinary conversation provides a powerful starting point for reconciling issues of curriculum with recent approaches to instruction. Older notions of learning emphasized specific content that was seen as "objective," and valuable for its own sake. Newer frameworks emphasize the situated nature of what we know: Specific content is seen to derive its meaning from the larger traditions of discourse in which it is embedded. As one consequence, the emphasis in discussions of teaching and learning has shifted toward the development of cognitive and linguistic processes that allow students to "construct meaning," to act and do (Anderson et al. 1994; Crusius 1991; Langer 1995; Seixas 1993; Spivey 1990; Wells and Chang-Wells 1992).

Curricular conversations are similarly *constructed* by their participants. The knowledge that evolves is knowledge that is socially negotiated through the process of conversation itself; it is knowledge-in-action. Taking conversation in its largest sense, this construction of knowledge involves readers and writers as well as speakers and listeners. Each text, whether spoken or written, is constructed by its authors and reinterpreted by the other participants. Written texts live long after their authors have left the conversation because this process of reconstrual allows texts to be made relevant in new contexts, by new participants. Without reconstrual, the texts would lose their voice and place within the ongoing conversation.

Individual traditions represent dynamic, changing ways of knowing and doing. In any living tradition, what is important is always in the process of being reassessed. Thus the science of the late 1990s is very different from that of the 1950s or even the 1980s, as are the history and the literature. The conversations that go on at all levels within these traditions change with time as new areas of inquiry open up and others are modified or abandoned. Even in our elementary schools, students today argue knowledgeably about gender stereotypes in the books they read, and about socially responsible forms of recycling and protection of the environment. Such discussions are central to contemporary traditions of literature, science, and social studies, but were hardly evident at all when these students' parents were in school. The topics of conversation have changed, but the essential process of learning to enter into culturally significant domains for conversation continues.

If the forms of curriculum discussed in the previous chapter are discussed in these terms, their essential weaknesses quickly become apparent. Bobbitt's (1924) lists of minimum essentials, for example, define a domain that consists of skills and types of knowledge that are unrelated to one another, and the teaching and learning processes associated with that domain reinforce their status as knowledge-out-of-context. The conversation that is supported within the domain will be limited and ritualistic, emphasizing presentation by the teacher and recitation by the student. Coherence, to the extent it occurs, will be procedural—generated by patterns of questioning (question, response, evaluation)—rather than thematic, arising out of the ebb and flow of authentic dialogue and debate. Describing Bobbitt's curriculum in these terms highlights its inadequacy as a domain for conversation, pushing us to develop curricula that are more likely to lead to the development of knowledge-in-action.

THE CONVERSATIONS THAT MATTER

Early in the twentieth century, the notion of an ongoing "Great Conversation" was taken up by liberal educationists working in an Arnoldian tradition. To men (and the spokespersons were all men) such as John Erskine (1948), Robert M. Hutchins (1952), and Mortimer Adler (1940), the "conversation" was a very specific, historical one, as reflected in the "great books" of Western culture.[1] Rather than offering alternative perspectives on the world, it offered one "true" vision. It was a narrow and elitist vision, but it did capture the way in which at least that one particular tradition with which the liberal educationists were concerned was a tradition of knowledge-in-action, in which the voices from the past spoke to issues and conditions of the present. Indeed, they argued for reading the Great Books without any background information, so that the reader could participate directly in the Great Conversation.

Today we recognize that there are many conversations, not one. They offer us alternative perspectives, new ways of knowing and doing, not a single set of truths winnowed by time. They speak in the voices of women as well as men, people of color as well as whites, the poor and marginalized as well as the privileged. All of these groups gain what they know through processes of "putting it into words," of taking

1. On the liberal education tradition, see Applebee 1974 and Russell 1991. In 1952, Hutchins and his colleagues published a fifty-four-volume set of Great Books of the Western World. Twentieth-century authors were not included, nor were women. Hutchins (1952) did acknowledge a second, Eastern tradition, but argued that it was necessary to understand our own tradition before we could hope to understand another (pp. 72–73).

action, within culturally constituted traditions of knowing and doing.

In introducing the notion of curriculum as a domain for conversation, I stated that the domains would represent "culturally significant" traditions of knowing and doing. This was a convenient shorthand for making the point that any curriculum is a *selection* that represents what a community believes is worthwhile. The notion that a particular community can determine what is worthwhile in curriculum can seem problematic in a diverse society such as the United States. But in a very real sense, the demands of the classroom force a coming-to-terms with the various cultural traditions that may be present. The nature of this coming-to-terms is highly political, reflecting the shifting relationships among the many groups in society at large. At times in U.S. history this has involved models of assimilation into a common "mainstream" tradition, or of a "melting pot" out of which a new common culture might emerge. Elements of these traditions remain in many schools today, but the dominant model at present seems to be one of seeking for commonalities while acknowledging differences. In ways unprecedented in the past, school curricula have begun to acknowledge the contributions of individuals from the variety of alternative traditions present within American society, in particular the contributions of women and of people of color, but also those of non-Western and other traditions that have been marginalized in the past. How these sometimes conflicting traditions can be reconciled within a curriculum remains problematic, however, and I will return to these issues in chapter 9.

LEARNING THROUGH CURRICULAR CONVERSATIONS

Knowledge-in-action is knowledge that is situated within traditions; if schools are to enable individuals to gain such knowledge, then we must consider how their entry into such traditions can best be facilitated. As students learn to act within the curricular domain, they simultaneously learn both the content and the tacit, socially constituted conventions that give shape and structure to the larger realms of discourse—they develop the knowledge-in-action that is the living tradition of discourse.

Domains for conversational action—curricula in the sense I am using here—are situated within (or across) larger traditions of discourse. The discussions of Shakespeare or Morrison or Marquez that take place in a classroom will be framed by larger traditions of literary study—by a sense of the field of English studies, and of the relationships between what students are doing and vital activity in that larger field. Because the conventions of discourse within the classroom are themselves constrained by the larger traditions of literary studies, in learning to participate in the conversational action of the classroom students are also learning to enter into the larger tradition. The rules of discourse within the larger universe set boundaries on permissible topics and ways of discussing that may not be immediately apparent in the conversation itself, just as the results of the conversation may have ramifications that echo far beyond its boundaries. Thus a discussion of a single text is likely to reflect larger patterns of what is considered discussable in literary studies, as well as of what are considered appropriate ways to discuss (forms of argument, types of evidence, patterns of thematization and topicality).

In the majority of English classrooms in the United States at the moment, the discussions that take place are framed by a tradition of New Critical commentary and analysis. This is the tradition in which most teachers were trained, and it still dominates in most high school and undergraduate English programs. In this tradition, discussion focuses on textual features and textual structure: It asks, in John Ciardi's words (1960), "How does a poem mean?" Out of this tradition, several generations of readers have learned to search for hidden meanings, to trace imagery and symbolism, and to talk of the unity and coherence of the verbal artifact. If we look into the typical classroom on any given day, these are the concerns that are likely to dominate discussion—because these are how the concerns of the larger field of English studies are interpreted

(Applebee 1993b; Huber 1992). (That these are no longer the concerns of many scholars in the field, and that the practices of the New Critics have themselves often been debased in practice, is another issue, one of teacher education and of professional discourse in the profession as a whole.)

A curricular conversation comprises a series of such discussions taking place over time—weeks or semesters or even years. As they continue to explore the domain, students come to be more effective participants in the larger conversation: Their contributions will grow in scope and complexity; their actions will be surer; their sense of mastery will increase. As they explore new aspects of the domain, their discoveries help them construe and reconstrue the domain as a whole. Engagement with new texts and new issues does not simply expand their knowledge of the tradition, but also casts light on texts and issues that have been discussed before.

CURRICULUM PLANNING

The problem of curriculum planning, then, is the problem of establishing a conversational domain and fostering relevant conversations within it. In a general sense, the conversational domains that are most important in American schools begin with the traditions of science, mathematics, social studies (particularly history, civics, and geography), and English studies. All of these, however, are very broad, and are made up of many more specialized traditions, in each of which the central conversations are always evolving and changing. As the larger conversation changes, the examples that are likely to be included within a curricular domain, as well as the kinds of discussions that are initiated around those examples, will change.

To take a specific example, the curriculum in virtually all American secondary schools and colleges includes a course in American literature. This course has its own history, articulating upward to larger traditions of discourse in literature and American studies, as well as to a tradition of discourse about civic virtue and nation-building. It became virtually universal after World War I, fueled by the patriotic fervor generated by the war and the emergence of American studies as an academic field of study (see Applebee 1974 on developments in the high school curriculum; Graff 1987 on the college). During the 1920s and 1930s it became institutionalized in its present form, as a chronological survey of works by major Americans. (Not, incidentally, as a course in major works by Americans; this resulted in the inclusion of many ephemeral works by Americans not known primarily for their writing.) As the course evolved over time, the conversations around which it was constituted began to lose their force. First, as the stresses of war became more distant, patriotism as a topic of conversation lost its ability to sustain extended discourse; later, the myths of the frontier and the peculiarly American spirit began to lose popularity. As the larger tradition of literary studies began to be dominated by the New Critics and to focus more sharply on the internal characteristics of individual works, rather than on the moral virtues they embodied or the cultural contexts they reflected, the works in the typical American literature survey course became less and less able to sustain interesting conversation. Recognizing that, critics who examined the high school curriculum from the perspective of English studies were calling for the elimination of a separate course in American literature as early as the 1960s (Lynch and Evans 1963). Their criticisms were ineffective, largely I think because the course has also continued to be perceived by the public at large—including the school boards that ultimately control the curriculum in U.S. schools—as a place to cultivate an American spirit. Whether such cultivation has been effective is another matter.

As a result, the American literature course has been in disarray for several decades, spending too much time on works that have had little interest for students, and lacking a living tradition of conversation into which students might enter. Only in the past few years has a tradition of discourse begun to develop in literary studies that in turn is revitalizing the conversation within some high school and college courses. This new tradition grows out of an awareness of the many strands of tradition that are woven through American history, and the ways in which they have interacted to determine whose voices would be heard, and whose wouldn't. Issues of gender, race, and class have become central to much of the discourse about literature, particularly as these issues have played out over time in American literature (see Lauter 1990; Greenblatt and Gunn 1992).

An Example: Creating a New Conversational Domain in an Introductory American Literature Course

Against this background, we can examine the curriculum of a fairly typical one-semester tenth-grade introductory American literature course as it evolved over several years. Its teacher, Tony Harrison, had taught for twenty-two years. Eleven of these had been in Riverhill, New Jersey, a large multiethnic school district known for its progressive philosophy. The course was one of a number that my colleagues and I examined as part of a study of curriculum decision-making in English (Applebee, Burroughs, and Stevens 1994).[2]

The course began with a curriculum structured around a coverage metaphor (from the Puritans to 1930) typical of such courses since their inception, but over several years evolved into a course in which Harrison sought to engage his students in a conversation about the nature of the voices in conflict in different periods of American history. The driving force behind these changes was a concern to broaden the multicultural content of the course.

The departmental syllabus called for the reading of a traditional canon in chronological order. It began with Puritan writers like Bradstreet and Edwards, moved to Hawthorne and Melville, and then to Twain, Crane, Wharton, Fitzgerald, and Steinbeck. In practice, the course was organized into five

2. The study focused on experienced and successful teachers of English and examined differences in curriculum between and among teachers, tracks, and schools. In this and later examples in this book, teachers are identified by pseudonyms.

units, each unit anchored by a novel: *The Scarlet Letter, Billy Budd, The Red Badge of Courage, Huckleberry Finn,* and *The Great Gatsby.* In early efforts to respond to multicultural issues, *Billy Budd* was replaced with *I Know Why the Caged Bird Sings, Huckleberry Finn* was dropped because of concerns about racism,[3] and an introductory unit on Native American literature was added.

Although the organization by novel allowed for some collateral reading of shorter pieces, Harrison found the scheme confining, especially given his sense of the importance of ethnic authors. In his first attempts to broaden the curriculum, he deemphasized the novels (they "take too much time") and added a variety of new, multicultural materials. These changes added breadth to the curriculum, but the multicultural materials remained as relatively isolated additions, rather than as integral parts of the course. As Harrison struggled with the problem of how to broaden the curriculum further, he began to organize the selections around the "clash of cultures." Class discussion, however, focused heavily on traditional methods of textual analysis rather than on the clash of cultures that was beginning to provide a new structuring principle.

In fact, clash of cultures opened up not just a different organizing principle, but also a new way to think about the focus of discussion. Gradually, Harrison began to think of the course as an exploration of the nature of the canon itself—issues that were simultaneously dominating debate within the larger tradition of literary study (e.g. Gates 1992). As he put it in an interview, the changes he introduced were largely in response to his own "desire to understand who chooses the literature." The shift in Harrison's conception of the course at this point is fundamental: He has moved from a conception of the curriculum in terms of coverage to one in terms of a significant set of conversations—there is a real issue of who chooses the

3. Debates about this book have led to its elimination from many school programs, often simply to avoid the possibility of controversy rather than because the issues have been well considered. Carey-Webb (1993) discusses the issues raised in teaching this book; Shaw (1994) reviews (unsympathetically) how the book has been discussed by literary critics.

canon, and with it the issue of what "American" literature really is. As this new conversation began to dominate Harrison's own thinking about the curriculum, he found it necessary to reconstruct the nature of the discussions as well. Rather than textual analysis, his classes began to talk about the conflicting cultures and ideas of each historical period.

There were some holdovers from earlier conversations even as the new domain was established, however, and these are instructive. With the two novels that his students had always most enjoyed—*The Scarlet Letter* and *The Great Gatsby*—Harrison continued to emphasize the analyses of structure and symbolism that he had used in the past. The students, however, felt the disjuncture between how these books were treated and the issues that dominated the rest of the course—and they rejected them because they were not construed as interesting in the context of the new conversation (even though both books had been class favorites in previous years, as part of a different conversation). In such circumstances, Harrison has a clear choice as the curriculum continues to evolve: to drop these two texts altogether, or to invite them into the new conversation (where both clearly could fit).

When Harrison began teaching the American literature course, classroom activities focused on clarifying plot and analyzing literary techniques, almost always through whole-class discussion. These emphases began to change as new issues began to emerge as topics for discussion. Fairly early in the change process, Harrison introduced role-playing activities, in which students acted out the divergent views of Native Americans and "New Arrivals," as reflected in selections from the Colonial period. Later in the process of change, he began to draw upon students' own experiences, as represented in their family stories. As he put it, "It is important to hear and share the voices of who we are, . . . the extraordinary richness of the traditions in this class." In the same spirit, he began to ask students to become experts on texts that the rest of the class had not read, partly to deal with the overwhelming amount of material that he was asking them to cope with, but also to allow discussion to play off what students thought was important.

Harrison's American literature class illustrates the close tie between the way that the curriculum is conceptualized and the way that instruction unfolds. When the class is seen primarily as a survey of the American canon, Harrison is comfortable leading students toward a shared understanding of canonical texts. When the class is seen as a domain for exploring the real issues surrounding where canons come from and the cultural conflicts that are apparent at any point in American literary history, Harrison begins to use activities that invite diverse interpretations and multiple points of view.

TRANSFORMING CURRICULUM

The argument in this chapter implies that schooling should be organized to help students enter into culturally significant domains for conversation, themselves representative of broader cultural traditions of knowing and doing. By placing the emphasis on *entry into* such conversations, I seek to ensure that students will emerge with knowledge-in-action rather than knowledge-out-of-context. By stressing *culturally significant* domains, I seek to ensure that education is organized around living traditions that look to the present and future as well as the past. And by stressing *domains for conversation,* I seek to ensure that there is an emphasis on the structure and interrelatedness of ideas and experiences within a domain. Each of these is a significant change in emphasis from current educational practice; together they offer the possibility of a significant transformation in the way schooling functions.

In most American schools and colleges, broad decisions about curriculum are influenced by factors that are beyond the control of the individual teacher. The expectations of the larger community ensure that subjects such as English, mathematics, science, and history are offered everywhere; such mandates are often a matter of law or accreditation standards as well as tradition. In the majority of schools and colleges, curriculum is also constrained by limits on resources. At times courses are offered because students must have them to fulfill graduation requirements, and materials are sometimes chosen simply because they are available, even if they seem inappropriate. This predicament is one that has faced most teachers at one time or another, and that faces many teachers all the time.

But institutional constraints on subjects and materials may be less critical than the teacher's decisions about the conversations in which students will be asked to engage. Materials that are less than ideal can be transformed when embedded in a new conversational domain, and the "best" materials can be stripped of their interest if they are not made a part of a living tradition of conversation, one that will sustain competing interpretations, exploration, and debate. In this chapter, we saw such processes at work in Tony Harrison's Introduction to American Literature course. Although he added new materials, the major transformation that he made was in his initial sense of what the course was really about—that is, he refocused the conversational domain. By shifting the organizing topic, he transformed the domain, and in doing so he revived his own interest as well as that of his students. And it is not accidental that in shifting the topic, he brought the course into better alignment with a larger, living tradition of discourse about American literature.

If curricula are to be transformed to support students' entry into significant domains for conversation, however, we need a better understanding of what such curricula might look like. Developing that understanding will be the task of the next chapters.

Characteristics of Effective Curricula

Treating curriculum as a domain for conversation leads to a new set of considerations in curriculum planning. What do effective curricula look like? How can they be shaped to foster sustained conversation? These are the questions that will be addressed in this and the following chapter.

In thinking about effective curricula, it is important to note that curriculum is established at many levels, from daily lessons to comprehensive programs that extend across years of study. My discussion focuses for the most part on the curriculum of the individual course, which is the level at which curriculum planning and debate usually take place in American middle and high schools. At the elementary school level, a similar set of debates focuses on the organization of subject area material within each given grade level (see, for example, Walmsley 1994). At the college level, course content is more likely to be the prerogative of the individual professor, and debates about curriculum structure are cast more broadly, about what courses to teach and what relationships, if any, there should be among them (see Graff 1992). These are at best rough characterizations, however, and the issues regularly spill over from one level to another. The curriculum in the freshman composition course at the University of Texas at Austin, for example, has become a part of the national debate about political correctness, while the call for state and national curricula embodied in the Goals 2000: Educate America Act of 1994 has generated public debate about the nature of the K–12 curriculum in each of the major school subjects.

Curriculum planning is usually approached as an exercise in domain specification and task analysis. That is, it begins with an inventory of important skills and concepts, and then moves on to arrange them in logical or psychological order. Taking curriculum as a domain for conversation, however, suggests a different starting point. Rather than beginning with an exhaustive inventory of the structure of the subject matter, we begin with a consideration of the conversations that matter—with traditions and the debates within them that enliven contemporary civilization. The question then becomes, how can we orchestrate these conversations so that students can enter into them?

H. P. Grice, a philosopher of language, provides a useful starting point in thinking about the features of an engaging and well-orchestrated curricular conversation. Grice notes that effective conversations are guided by "a common purpose or set of purposes, or at least a mutually accepted direction. This purpose or direction may be fixed from the start (e.g., by an initial proposal of a question for discussion), or it may evolve during the exchange. . . ." (Grice 1975, p. 45). In a curricular conversation, those purposes will be constrained by the larger field or subject within which the conversation is located (e.g., science or literature or home economics), but other details of the conversation may either be set by the teacher or negotiated (Mayher 1990) as the conversation evolves.

If the conversation is to be effective, all participants must honor a tacit agreement to cooperate in carrying the conversation forward rather than to obstruct or interrupt it. This is Grice's Cooperative Principle, and its conditions are as essential to an effective curricular conversation as they are in any other conversational situation. Effective conversations may reflect heated disagreement or quiet consensus, but they continue to work only as long as the various contributions are relevant to the common direction or purposes. (It is interesting that common usage refers to troublesome students as "disruptive" or "uncooperative," labels that provide particularly apt descriptions of their effect on curricular conversations.)

A curriculum that is cooperative and effective in a Gricean

sense has four important characteristics.[1] These have to do with the *quality, quantity,* and *relatedness* of the topics of conversation, and the *manner* in which the conversation is carried forward. These characteristics, which can be thought of as principles of effective conversation, can be applied both to the moment-to-moment interaction that Grice originally analyzed, and to the larger curricular conversation that stretches over time and space. Since it is the latter with which I am most concerned here, I will reserve "conversation" for discussions of curriculum as it evolves over more extended periods of time, and use "discussion" when I am referring to specific classroom interactions (that is, to what Tharp and Gallimore [1988] have called "instructional conversations," the moment-to-moment interactions during which teaching and learning occur).

The four characteristics of effective curricular conversations will be discussed in turn.

Quality: An Effective Curriculum Is Built around Language Episodes of High Quality

The quality of language episodes in a curricular conversation has at least two aspects. First and foremost, contributions to the conversation must be clear and accurate, supported where appropriate by relevant argument and evidence. This seems a straightforward enough requirement, yet in fact it is more complicated to accomplish than it might seem. The state of Texas, for example, has recently learned how difficult it is even to insist that science and social studies materials contain no errors of fact. When it forced textbook companies to make extensive and expensive changes to books submitted for adoption, it found some companies decided to withdraw from the

---

1. The four principles that follow derive directly from Grice's four conversational maxims. They are recast and clarified here in terms of curricular issues, based on our studies of the evolution of curriculum in particular classrooms (Applebee, Burroughs, and Stevens 1994).

Texas market—limiting rather than expanding the options available to Texas teachers.

At a more difficult level, quality is always a function of the larger traditions within which curriculum is embedded. As knowledge is reformulated and the central arguments within a discipline change, the quality of particular ideas and contributions is continually reassessed. This has always been evident in fields like the sciences, where popular conceptions of scientific progress imply that knowledge will be rapidly out of date and thus textbooks in need of constant revision. But it is equally true in other subjects. In English studies, for example, as well as in reading and language arts, curriculum has changed over the past twenty years in response to questions about fairness and accuracy in the depiction of women and minorities. *How* the curriculum should be construed in order to effectively reflect those contributions, however, has been a matter of continuing and still-unresolved debate (Minnich 1990). (Indeed, the "canon controversy" has become a minor industry, spawning myriad books, conferences, and reports in the popular press. See, among many others, Banks 1993; Gates 1992; Graff 1992; Purves 1993; Scholes 1991; Shaw 1994.) On a different level, judgments of quality may change depending on how a work is contextualized: How do we treat a book such as *The Education of Little Tree,* when we discover that its author, rather than being a Native American, was a leader in the Ku Klux Klan? What sort of reassessment do we make of Thomas Jefferson's writings on freedom and democracy, in light of his own status as a slaveholder? Such questions (which of course may become part of the curricular conversation itself) all have to do with judgments about the quality of episodes within a particular conversational domain.

Another aspect of quality has to do with the ability of the material introduced to support meaningful conversation. Episodes of high quality require materials that will sustain substantive discussion—there has to be something to say that is relevant to the general purposes and direction of the conversation. One of the characteristics of mediocre and second-rate materials is that they are too transparent or too thin to support much discussion or debate. In English studies, for example, there are many examples of popular novels and poetry that students find accessible and interesting to read on their own. (In a recent survey, titles by Judy Blume and Stephen King led non-college-bound seniors' lists of personally significant titles; Applebee 1993b.) When they are brought into the classroom, however (as they sometimes are to encourage "reluctant" readers or "motivate" uninterested students), there may be little there to sustain conversation. Instruction is then likely to deteriorate into vocabulary development and reading practice, because there is little else to do with the text. Teachers sometimes reach out to the mediocre and second rate in the hope of responding directly to students' interests, only to grow frustrated when they and their classes discover together how little there may be to say about it. (For a trenchant critique of materials selected for relevance to immediate interests at the expense of quality, see Lynch and Evans 1963.) Student interest and quality of materials do not need to stand in tension with one another, but too often teachers have treated them as though such tension were inevitable.

Even with formulaic texts, issues of quality have to do with the conversation within which the texts are embedded. Such texts might provoke extended discussion in conversations about gender roles in society at large, for example, or about the role of formula plots in recreational reading. Such conversations, however, are quite different from the ones intended by the authors, or from those likely to result from including such titles in an attempt to motivate reluctant students or to respond to their interests.

As these examples suggest, quality is not an absolute; it is always defined with respect to a particular topic of conversation. Looking at quality in this way adds an interesting twist to some of the more public debates about the quality of the curriculum in American schools. For the most part, attacks on quality are really debates about which conversations students should engage in. When the quality of a book is questioned, it is usually because of objections to the conversations the book might provoke. Given the conflicting traditions that are part of American society—a topic that I will return to in chapter 9—controversies about the curriculum may be inevitable. They show themselves most vividly in public debates about the inclusion or exclusion of particular books or about the handling of topics such as evolution and creationism, but they may be even more widespread in the self-censorship that leads a teacher or department simply to avoid some topics of conversation altogether (DelFattore 1992; Moffett 1988).

Because traditions of discourse change, judgments of quality are likely to change with them. To continue the example introduced in chapter 4, many of the materials in the chronologically organized high school course in American literature were of appropriate quality as part of a conversation about patriotism and the moral values of prominent early Americans. They became less appropriate, and less able to sustain discourse, as the conversations of most interest within literary studies began to change. Short excerpts were particularly vulnerable to such shifts: However illustrative they must once have seemed in conversations about great Americans, they were of little use in New Critical conversations that emphasized the structural integrity of works as a whole. Thus the use of excerpts, like the choice of selections for their relevance to adolescent interests, drew particularly scathing criticism from New Critics like James Lynch and Bertrand Evans (1963).

QUANTITY: AN EFFECTIVE CURRICULUM HAS AN APPROPRIATE BREADTH OF MATERIALS TO SUSTAIN CONVERSATION

The essence of conversation is that it must allow interaction: among teacher and students, among students, among students and the texts they read or watch or listen to. If there is too much material to cover—and pressure for coverage is usually the villain here—dialogue is almost of necessity supplanted by monologue, in which the teacher reverts to telling students what they need to know. (Bakhtin [1981] calls pure monologue "pedagogical" discourse, an ascription which is an unfortunately accurate characterization of much of education.)

There is a version of the argument for coverage before conversation that can be particularly seductive in some subject areas, particularly the hard sciences. This is the argument that in a completely new domain, students don't know "enough" to take independent action. In chapter 8 I will return to the issue of how instruction can be designed to support such action. The point here is a simple one: If we do not structure the curricular domain so that students can actively enter the discourse, the knowledge they gain will remain decontextualized and unproductive. They may succeed on a limited spectrum of school tasks that require knowledge-out-of-context, but they will not gain the knowledge-in-action that will allow them to become active participants in the discourse of the field.

Conversations can also be thwarted by too little material, however. In the interests of time and coverage, lessons are sometimes orchestrated around "representative" or "typical" material, selected because it captures some essential features of the topic under discussion. Thus in the original version of Tony Harrison's course, each novel was chosen to represent a particular era in American literary history. *Billy Budd,* for example, was initially selected as an example of Transcendentalism, and *The Great Gatsby* as an example of the modern period. Such materials are really only illustrations in an educational monologue. Students can match the illustrations against whatever points the teacher or the textbook makes, but the illustrations do not provide students with enough substance to make their own generalizations about the periods in question. (One result of the lack of material to build upon is that such courses usually end up talking about other issues—in Harrison's case, focusing on textual analysis rather than on chronological and stylistic relationships.) There are times, of course, when such "mentioning" by the teacher or textbook may be all that is desired, but the knowledge that results should not be confused with the knowledge-in-action that real conversation engenders.

Pressures for coverage come from many directions. State legislatures and local school boards, when they become involved in curriculum, are more likely to compromise on the side of inclusiveness rather than selectivity: When one is pressed by special interest groups, it is easier to include something for everyone than to make hard choices about how much material is really manageable or which conversations are most important. The recent attempts to generate national curriculum standards in major subject areas, for example, have been easy targets for such critiques. The American history standards produced by a federally funded standards project in 1994 were quickly criticized for not explicitly mentioning Robert E. Lee, Paul Revere, or Thomas Edison. Less attention was given to the avowed goals of involving students in "great issues, debates, and developments" (Nash and Crabtree 1994), by asking, for example, "Was it right . . . for Lincoln, in his Emancipation Proclamation, to free only those slaves behind the Confederate lines?" (Gugliotta 1994). Though a more inclusive catalog of names would arguably have led to a more superficial and thus less effective curriculum, one that placed more emphasis on knowledge-out-of-context and less on knowledge-in-action, the criticism was withering and eventually led to condemnation of the standards by a near-unanimous vote of the U.S. Senate.[2]

For students, too much coverage quickly reduces a course to an exercise in memorization without the opportunity to take action on their own. For teachers, and more particularly for textbooks, the attempt to cover too much produces a curriculum that is bereft of the focus that should give life to the study of any subject.

2. See, for example, Lynne Cheney's attack (1994) and the subsequent rebuttal by Nash and Crabtree (1994). Although much of the argument turned on numbers, the numbers were simply ammunition in a larger debate about how history was to be construed. The critics charged the standards with an overemphasis on inclusiveness and on the abuses of western European colonization. Nash and Crabtree, responding as codirectors of the project, said they were simply providing "accurate history, for any history that ignores large parts of American society is incomplete and therefore distorted." The Senate resolution condemned the standards and proclaimed that any recipient of federal funds for the development of national teaching standards "should have a decent respect for the contributions of Western civilization and United States history, ideas, and institutions." (*Wall Street Journal* 1995).

Violations of the principles of appropriate quantity and quality are apparent in recent school textbooks across a variety of subject areas. David Elliott and Arthur Woodward (1990) comment on the problems:

> Chief among the shortcomings researchers have identified are "mentioning," or shallow coverage of a wide range of topics; "inconsiderateness," or poor writing; emphasis on lower-level memorizing of facts and generalizations to the exclusion of problem solving and other higher-order cognitive processes; the avoidance of important topics because some consider them too controversial; and failure to promote adequate understanding of the real nature of knowledge fields, such as science and history, that are the bases of school subjects. (P. 223)

One of the dangers with such curricula is that the resulting conversation will be so unengaging that students will turn away from the subject altogether.

RELATEDNESS: THE PARTS
OF AN EFFECTIVE CURRICULUM
ARE INTERRELATED

One of the most important features of effective domains for conversation is the sense of relatedness among the parts. It is this that makes cumulative conversations possible, and that provides a sense of direction to what has been covered and what remains to come. If the parts are not sufficiently related, the conversation will fragment, forced to separate and start over each time something new is introduced.

Unfortunately, English studies have a long-standing predisposition to come unglued—to separate into the myriad individual studies from which they were assembled at the turn of the century (grammar, reading, literary history, spelling, philology, oratory, and composition, among others). They also have a tendency to absorb any new activity that may be proposed, simply on the grounds that in one way or another the activity involves language. Thus we teach students in elementary and secondary school how to run a spell check on their word processor, make introductions, answer the telephone, write thank-you letters, criticize advertisements, analyze rap lyrics, write reports for science and social studies, ad infinitum—with little sense of what is central and what is peripheral to our classes or to our subject area. While each such activity may be perfectly reasonable in its own right, together they do not constitute a curricular domain.

At the college level a similar kind of fragmentation occurs between courses. In English, for example, there are usually separate courses that deal with writing, with literature, with popular culture, and with writing in or across the disciplines. There may also be separate courses in linguistics or rhetoric. Fragmentation extends beyond these broad areas, however, so that even within a field such as literature, different courses will represent different traditions of criticism and scholarship. New Critical standards of textual analysis exist next to those that emphasize deconstruction, feminist criticism, and cultural studies, comfortably isolated by the fault lines between courses in the catalog. In most departments, such relationships as there are among courses are established artificially through prerequisites, requirements for the major, or emphases on a comprehensive exam. As Gerald Graff has argued (1987), the emphasis on field coverage reflected in such arrangements has been a convenient institutional expedient that allows departments to assimilate a variety of conflicting traditions while avoiding the conflict that real dialogue among them might produce. The lack of dialogue, however, has in turn led to stagnation and loss of vitality in each of the separate traditions.

In elementary and secondary schools, thematic teaching has been one traditional way to ensure that the various parts of a curriculum are related in a more or less integral fashion. In theory, a theme establishes a unified topic of conversation that is then explored through a variety of interrelated activities. The activities are intended to enrich students' understanding of the overall theme, and the theme in turn to add interest and provide a sense of direction to the individual activities. In practice, however, we have as a profession given surprisingly little attention to how to construct effective thematic units, or to the kinds of relatedness that will in fact foster rich conversations (on the problems and possibilities in themes, see Lipson, Valencia, Wixson, and Peters 1993; Walmsley 1994). The activities gathered together around many themes are at best superficial: They result from brainstorming about "related" activities without a reweaving of the result into a conversational whole. Thus we may question whether students' first encounters with Shakespeare will necessarily benefit from building a model of the Globe Theater, or whether a classroom collection of teddy bears brought from home will add depth to a discussion of *Ira Sleeps Over,* simply because Ira happens to have a teddy bear (Silva and Delgado-Larocco 1993).

Even when new activities and materials are added to a curriculum for good reasons, the principle of relatedness may require a thorough recasting of the conversational domain before the new additions become effective. In classrooms I have studied, this has been particularly evident when teachers have begun to broaden their curriculum to include more multicultural materials. These noncanonical materials, almost by definition, do not fit well into traditional analyses of historical periods, literary devices, major genres, or even familiar themes; if they are to be something more than a part of an awkward mosaic, such works require a reconstrual of the domain itself.

We have already seen this process at work in Tony Harrison's reworking of the curriculum for his tenth-grade Introduction to American Literature. Warren Rosenberg, a professor at Wabash College, provides a similar example at the college level. In an article (1990) about his own attempts at curriculum revision, he recounts the frustration that developed when he first added Harriet A. Jacobs's *Incidents in the Life of a Slave Girl* to an American literature course he was teaching. Positioned between Melville's "Benito Cereno" and Whitman's poetry, Jacobs's text did not fit into the pattern of conversation the students had come to expect. "Following the densely structured and linguistically assured 'Benito Cereno' in the syllabus, Jacobs's book looked simplistic, episodic, uneven, unstructured; presented without any explanatory defense, she didn't have a chance against the major canonical writers" (p. 136). Rosenberg's students wondered if a slave could have written the book herself; and even if she had, why they should waste their time on an unknown author. In later versions of the curriculum, Rosenberg redefined the conversational domain to include an examination of the process of canon formation, and of the social and cultural forces that determined which authors were valued and which were not. Only in this context did Jacobs's work begin to feel "cooperative" and the syllabus coherent; in fact Rosenberg notes that students "now generally . . . see Jacobs's text as appropriate and even necessary to the course" (p. 145).

MANNER: INSTRUCTION IS GEARED TO HELPING STUDENTS ENTER INTO THE CURRICULAR CONVERSATION

What we learn is in large part a function of how we learn it. If students are in fact to learn to enter into culturally significant domains for conversation, instruction must enable and support that participation. Only through participation guided by others will students develop the knowledge-in-action that will enable them to participate effectively on their own.

A pedagogy that supports students' entry into meaningful traditions of conversation is of necessity dialogic. It is dependent on responsive interaction that both anticipates and provokes the reply that is forthcoming. As Bakhtin puts it (1981) in discussing language more generally,

> the word in living conversation is directly, blatantly, oriented toward a future answer-word: it provides an answer, anticipates it and structures itself in the answer's direction. Forming itself in an atmosphere of the already spoken, the word is at the same time determined by that which has not yet been said but which is needed and in fact anticipated by the an-

swering word. Such is the situation in any living dialogue. (P. 280)

Effective pedagogies build upon this elemental link between a word and its anticipated response. The teacher's comment is linked to an anticipation of how the student will respond just as tightly as the student's is linked to an anticipation of the teacher's reaction. It is a part of their cooperation as they explore issues within the conversational domain that has been established, as both use their understandings of past interchanges and their predictions of future responses to carry the conversation forward. The discussions that result are open-ended: The topics that are discussed, the degree of consensus and of disagreement, will be negotiated among the participants as the conversation evolves. Students will talk with one another, as well as with the teacher, and their contributions will be treated as enriching, rather than derailing, the conversation. The teacher will continue to be central and authoritative, but not authoritarian. Like the master artisan, the teacher will mediate between the classroom discussion and the larger tradition of discourse in which it is subsumed.

Judith Langer and I have discussed the features of such learning environments under the general rubric of *instructional scaffolding* (Applebee and Langer 1983; Langer and Applebee 1986, 1987; Langer 1991, 1995; Roberts and Langer 1991), and our work is part of a much larger universe of research aimed at developing a more effective pedagogy for knowledge-in-action (e.g., Cazden 1979; Eeds and Wells 1989; Goldenberg 1992/93; Palincsar and Brown 1984; Rogoff and Gardner 1984; Rogoff 1990; Wells and Chang-Wells 1992). This work has focused on such characteristics as allowing students room to develop their own understandings in their reading and writing; ensuring that activities support natural processes of thought and language; and in turn helping students internalize a repertoire of effective strategies of language and thought that they can use in new contexts. All of these features can be thought of as preconditions for dialogue in which students can both participate and, through that participation, gain the knowledge-in-action that will allow them to participate more fully on their own.

I will return to the nature of a pedagogy to support conversational action in chapter 8. For now, it is worth noting that it is here, in the manner of instruction, that a reconceptualization of curriculum as culturally significant domains for conversation reconnects with recent work in constructivist pedagogy, offering the possibility of developing a unified theory of curriculum and instruction.

ONE CONVERSATION OR MANY?

Most fields of study are not neat and tidy, with one dominant conversation in which everyone participates happily. Disciplines are more like societies than communities; they are built out of many different local conversations, with different histories and major participants, often in competition for status and position within the field (Prior 1994). Some of these conversations may share a governing idea that allows (or is the result of) cross-fertilization; constructivism, for example, has had a widespread influence on fields as diverse as philosophy, psychology, and the history of science. Others (like many of the debates within graduate English studies in the 1970s and 1980s) may be at odds with one another, best encompassed perhaps in Gerald Graff's proposal (1992) that curriculum be organized to introduce students to the central conflicts within the field. Still others may be so far apart that they simply talk past one another (as often seems to be the case between Freudians and cognitivists in psychology).

As we think about curriculum as it plays itself out across courses and years, the relationships among such conversations become increasingly important. The idea of education as one great conversation has always had an appeal. It was argued explicitly by liberal educators in the Arnoldian tradition—who went so far as to provide a chronological curriculum for a lifetime of reading in the Western tradition (Hutchins 1952). It has also been argued by progressive educators seeking to integrate or correlate curriculum across subject areas, and to provide students with a unified vision of the world (on earlier proposals, see Applebee 1974 and Graff 1992). The problem in such proposals has usually been that in looking for commonalities across traditions of discourse, they have lost sight of the differences that are also part of their richness and appeal. Conversations about literature are, ultimately, different than those about history, and both are different from conversations about science, however fruitful cross-fertilization among traditions may be. When they are brought together, as they have been at various points in American education, something of value may be lost even as other things of value are gained. (English teachers in the Progressive Era, for example, usually found themselves subsumed into conversations of interest to science or history, rather than engaged in some new, greater conversation that drew in unique ways on each of the disciplines.) There is a place for disciplinary as well as interdisciplinary conversations, and the continuing problem for schools and colleges is to find the most productive balance among them. In planning curriculum, whether within or between disciplines, we need to remember that judgments about quality and relatedness will be affected by the conversations we choose to encourage, and that issues of quantity of material will quickly surface if the topics become too broad. It may also help to remind ourselves that the richness of interdisciplinary work comes from the expertise, the knowledge-in-action, that arises out of prior immersion within a particular discipline.

Structuring Curricular
Conversations

Curricular conversations are meant to be occasions for learning; although not spontaneous, they can be engaging. The topic of conversation is usually introduced by the teacher, but the details of the curriculum may be negotiated among the class participants. (Even the most comprehensive proposals for a fully negotiated curriculum begin with a general direction for conversation, even if it is as broad as "the teaching of English" or "contemporary literature"; see Mayher 1990, pp. 263ff.) As the curriculum evolves (whether planned by the teacher or negotiated with the students), some things will be singled out as more central and others as less so, and relationships among the parts will be sketched out or clarified. As Tony Harrison revised the curriculum for the Introduction to American Literature course discussed in chapter 4, for example, he selected new texts both to represent particular chronological periods and to reflect across-period strands of work by authors from particular racial or ethnic groups. These relationships provided starting points for the conversations that took place in his class, and thus for what his students learned. In general, the way we structure the curriculum—the experiences that are included and the relationships that are or can be established among them—will shape the kinds of knowledge-in-action that students develop. At the beginning, their understanding of the conversational domain may be partial and incomplete, but it will grow as the conversation continues.

In this chapter, I want to examine the kinds of structure that may exist within a curriculum and the extent to which different structures tend to support or inhibit the development of conversation. In practice, such structures exist at several different levels. To use a common distinction, there is the formal curriculum as represented in lesson plans, syllabi, textbooks, or official curriculum guidelines; the enacted curriculum, which represents the transformations that take place because of the teachers' and students' interactions around the formal curriculum; and the received curriculum, which reflects how students make sense of the curricular conversations in which they are engaged. Different curriculum structures may occur at each of these levels, structures that may be more or less supportive of evolving conversations, and in turn of the development of knowledge-in-action.

Structure emerges in two ways. On the one hand, a curriculum is likely to have an organizing topic or question that sets the initial direction of the conversation. This overall topic provides a sense of what is central and what is more peripheral to the domain. The topic of a curricular domain can be very concrete: The topic of a handwriting curriculum, for example, is a set of particular written representations of the twenty-six capital and lowercase letters. The topic can also be abstract and conceptual, as in a literature curriculum centered on literature as the realization of social and cultural conditions at a particular place and time. Once a topic has been established, some material becomes more central and other material less central to the conversational domain—and some will simply be irrelevant. A first pass at these judgments of relevance will be part of the formal curriculum, but they will continue to evolve in response to the interests and knowledge of each group of students.

The second aspect of structure involves the relationships among the parts. Again, these relationships can range from concrete and perceptual to abstract and conceptual; they include such familiar structuring devices as chronology, taxonomy, causality, similarity, difference, and complementarity. These devices operate in different ways on the different levels of the curriculum introduced earlier. In the formal curriculum, for example, such devices may be used by curriculum planners as organizing devices that help them "parse" the domain and ensure that significant ideas are represented. In the enacted curriculum, on the other hand, these same kinds of relationships may become intellectual tools used by the teacher and the students to seek out relationships and enrich the web of meaning they are developing. Given an experience, they can search for its causes, note its similarities to and differences from other things with which they are familiar, and classify it hierarchically or taxonomically as part of a larger system. In this way, the conversation that takes place within a domain may discover more relationships than the formal curriculum specified. Conversely, if the conversation that is enacted does not address them, relationships that were important in developing a formal curriculum may never be noticed by students.

These two types of structural relationships underlie a wide variety of different curriculum structures, some of which *by virtue of their structure* are more supportive of conversation than are others,[1] and thus more supportive of the development of knowledge-in-action that participation in curricular conversations can foster. A few common structures are discussed below. A real curriculum may end up with a structure that is a complex hybrid of several of these types, but they help us understand some of the alternatives and the implications of emphasizing one or another of them.

CATALOG

Some formal curricula simply *catalog* items or experiences, with no further links among the parts. Such a curriculum has no real topic or direction, only a diffuse and unspecified sense of a domain. This kind of structure is surprisingly prevalent. We have seen it already in the titles on the college entrance lists from the turn of the century, as well as in the functional skills that were enumerated by Franklin Bobbitt (1924) and

1. The problem of structure is a general one that extends across many aspects of human experience. The analysis that follows parallels Vygotsky's discussion of concept development (1962) and my own application of that analysis to the structure of children's storytelling (Applebee 1978). In all three cases, there is a trade-off between the difficulty in managing an increasingly complex cognitive structure (or amount of relatedness) and the ability to organize increasing amounts of ideas or information that such structure provides.

his descendants. E. D. Hirsch's recent (1987) delineation of knowledge necessary for cultural literacy represents a similar catalog, in its lengthy alphabetical lists of terms that students should know.

Because there are no conceptual links within the domain described by such catalogs, the domain itself is likely to remain indeterminate. The structure of such a curriculum offers nothing to help the teacher and students sustain their conversations because each new element requires starting over—there are by definition no relationships among the parts. When such structures are used to organize a course or a strand of material within it, the result is usually that instruction remains at the level of memorization and recitation detached from meaningful context. Teachers often try to make such practice interesting by embedding the practice in more meaningful contexts—for example, by asking students to write a paragraph or two in which all of their weekly vocabulary words are successfully embedded—but the structure of the curriculum itself militates against the development of knowledge-in-action.

Catalogs are also frequently used to organize larger units of coursework, most notably at the college level. Like the catalog structure of a single course, the catalog organization of sets of courses works against attempts at broader conversations. While individual courses may be challenging and rewarding, links across them are at best fortuitous. Gerald Graff has commented (1992) on the lack of community—and of conversation—that this engenders:

> One of the oddest things about the university is that it calls itself a community of scholars yet organizes its curriculum in a way that conceals the links of the community from those who are not already aware of them. The courses being given at any moment on a campus represent any number of rich potential conversations within and across disciplines. But since students experience these conversations only as a series of monologues, the conversations become actual

only for the minority who can reconstruct them on their own. (P. 106)

An Example of a Catalog: English One Day at a Time

To gain a better sense of what happens when a curriculum uses a catalog structure, I want to turn to another example from my recent study of curricular decision-making (Applebee, Burroughs, and Stevens 1994), in this case the curriculum in an English course for ninth-grade lower-track students. Zach Williams, who taught the course, was highly regarded in his upstate New York district, which served a multiracial population of the urban poor. Williams had taught for seven years at the time we met him, but his ninth-grade class at Lexington High School was a difficult one: The students were generally uninterested in school, and absenteeism and turnover on the class register were high.

In Williams's class, the curriculum consisted of a series of reading selections dealing with social issues that might be of interest to young adults. The books Williams selected were chosen from a departmental list that Williams had evaluated as "horrible" and in desperate need of new titles. But as often happens there was little time to review possible replacement titles, and money to buy them was scarce. He ended up choosing five texts: Paul Zindel's *The Pigman,* William Armstrong's *Sounder,* Gloria Miklowitz's *After the Bomb,* S. E. Hinton's *Rumblefish,* and Irene Hunt's *The Lottery Rose.* Williams augmented the novels with some shorter readings, particularly from Scholastic *Scope,* which were about contemporary issues.

Neither Williams nor his students saw any overt connections among the course readings, beyond a vague sense of a common set of selection criteria. As one student explained, Williams "probably picked them because he thinks they are good." Williams himself said that continuity in his course lay in the skills he sought to foster: reading comprehension, coherence in writing, a willingness to get involved in life. Beyond that, he admitted, "there is no continuity."

In fact, the lack of larger structure in Williams's curriculum was a deliberate strategy for dealing with the problems of his lower track classes. Faced with poor attendance and high dropout rates, Williams concentrated "on getting something done in each period that doesn't depend on the kid having been there the previous period." Because most of the students were poor readers, he spent a good deal of time reading the required texts aloud to them, modeling intonation and phrasing. Discussion activities and writing (primarily reader-response journals) were in turn related to material covered in these read-aloud sessions, breaking down even the book-length works into relatively independent daily segments that could be handled by whoever happened to show up for class.

At one level, this approach to curriculum accomplished what Williams had intended. Students had a "fresh start" each day, and absences and new students caused little disruption. At another level, however, both Williams and his students found the class to be a real struggle. The fresh start each day kept any continuing conversation from developing, and neither Williams nor his students had a sense of what was likely to happen next. Because there was no continuity, Williams had to initiate a new conversation each day, and could not rely even on the students who had been there the day before to help him.

COLLECTION

Another type of curriculum structure evolves from identifying a topic and choosing elements to explore based on a sense of "set-ness" (Great Books, Modes of Discourse, Systems of the Body). The result is a *collection*. With some relatively well-defined topics (for example, Modes of Discourse), the result over a period of time may be relatively taxonomic, particularly if the exploration remains at a high enough level of abstraction (narration, description, argument, and poetry, for example, rather than the virtually infinite uses of language).

For other topics (e.g., Great Books), the collection that results is likely to be more of a sampler than a taxonomy.

A collection structure is often used to link individual units that focus on separate parts of the collection (on the characteristics of argument, say). While extended conversation may develop within the individual units, the structure provides little guidance for conversation across units (about relationships between argument and narration, for example). Explorations of such links among the parts of the collection will be fortuitous rather than expected, since the elements are chosen to complete the collection rather than because of relationships that are perceived among them. A formal curriculum that is no more than a collection may of course be transformed by teacher and students as they construct relationships and impose a coherence on the enacted or received curriculum that may be more fully developed than those that guided the initial construction of the formal curriculum.

The collection is a very common curriculum structure in American schools. Literature courses through grade 10 are typically organized by themes or genres that are "sampled" in isolation rather than being related one to another. (At the college level, similar collections are evident in separate courses based on genres or authors.) Writing courses are typically organized around types of discourse, each of which is explored separately before moving on to another part of the domain. In other subject areas, geography courses are sometimes organized around the major continents each visited in turn, biology courses around systems of the body, and foreign language courses around verb tenses.

SEQUENTIAL

Some collections have an internal order based on chronology or hierarchy (e.g., of difficulty, complexity, or value). In the simplest examples of such *sequential* curricula, sequence may provide the only organizing principle. Works in a literature class may be sequenced by the dates they were written, just as the kings and queens of England may be studied in the order of their reigns. Sequence can also be hierarchical, as in composition curricula that move from the study of sentences to paragraphs and finally to whole essays, or in social studies courses that move from the family to the community to the nation.

The purely sequential curriculum, like the catalog, provides little structural support for conversation to develop. The elements sit in a fixed and relatively narrow relationship to one another, and the organization of the course provides little help in constructing further meaning. Such curricula are a relatively common byproduct of an atomistic approach to curriculum planning. They result in well-structured scope and sequence charts in which the sequencing principle usurps any other focus. (At the college level, a concern with sequence is apparent when separate courses focus on major literary periods—but the sequence disappears in the enacted curriculum since students can usually take such courses in any order they choose.) As a result, students may develop knowledge about the materials they are studying, but not the knowledge-in-action that comes only from real exploration of the relationships among them.

An Example: British Literature
in Sequence

For an example of a typical sequentially organized curriculum, we can examine Claudia Callahan's junior/senior course in British literature at Riverhill High School. Callahan had seventeen years of experience teaching high school English at the time we studied the curriculum in her course, and taught primarily honors and Advanced Placement courses.

The British Literature course was organized as a survey, and Callahan selected works to represent various literary periods. Though her approach was extensive it was not all-inclusive—she omitted authors and periods she did not know well, and concentrated on those she liked. The syllabus that resulted included excerpts from *Beowulf* and Chaucer; *Othello* (Shakespeare); *Gulliver's Travels* (Swift); the Romantic poets;

Hard Times (Dickens); *The Importance of Being Earnest* (Wilde); *Pygmalion* (Shaw); a collection of Christmas stories; *Dubliners* (Joyce); *The Loneliness of the Long-Distance Runner* (Sillitoe); a selection of contemporary poets; and *Family* (Emecheta). Because they ran out of time, the class never discussed the Sillitoe or the contemporary poetry.

The texts were for the most part arranged in chronological order, and Callahan certainly considered the course to offer a historical survey. Yet questions of history and period were addressed on an ad hoc basis rather than as part of a larger, continuing conversation. Instead, Callahan's emphases in each book tended to reflect her own experiences with them in university coursework. Topics that received considerable attention included use of language (*Beowulf, Canterbury Tales, Othello,* and "A Child's Christmas in Wales"); character analysis (*Canterbury Tales, Othello, Pygmalion,* and *Dubliners*); and genre analysis (*Beowulf, Gulliver's Travels, The Importance of Being Earnest,* "Christmas Morning," and *The Loneliness of the Long Distance Runner* [in prospect, even though there was no time for class discussion]).

The impact of these shifting conversations was that the enacted curriculum was essentially a catalog of "greatest hits" of British literature, with few connections perceived among them. In fact when we interviewed students about their experiences, they were not universally convinced that the course had been organized chronologically. That some students might not be aware of the chronological structure in a chronologically organized course surprised me at first, but I have since found that it can happen quite easily in survey courses. As in Callahan's case, chronology often ends up serving as a convenient selection device for the teacher, but not a significant part of class discussion or of a larger curricular conversation within which that discussion might be embedded. There is little discussion of sequence or historicity or periodization—nor, when only one or two works are read from any particular period, is there enough material for students to participate in such discussions intelligently even if the teacher initiates them. As a result many students pay little attention to the chronology, or miss it altogether. In this case the structure that organized the formal curriculum was at best a minor feature of the enacted curriculum; and for some of the students it was not part of the received curriculum at all.

EPISODIC

When a stronger sense of an overall topic is added to the ordering principle of a sequential curriculum, the curriculum structure becomes *episodic*. Conversations about chronologically organized literary texts, for example, may focus on literature as a reflection of its time. In such a course, each episode provides a new opportunity for participants to see this general principle at work. As conversations develop within an episodic curriculum, the structure leads students to return at regular intervals to the organizing topic, enriching and deepening their understanding of it. The limitation of the episodic curriculum, however, is that the different episodes are typically treated as casting light on the central topic but not on one another. The discussions that arise around the last episode are not related to those in the first; the structure that is present invites affirmation rather than reconstrual and reassessment of earlier experiences.

The episodic curriculum is also quite prevalent in American schools. It is easy to plan and teach, since each episode or segment flows logically from the previous ones yet remains self-contained; once the sequence is acknowledged, new episodes can be taken up and set aside without a great deal of attention to other episodes. Chronologically organized courses in history, art, and literature often take on an episodic structure, as the course turns from one period to the next without raising questions that cut across periods (e.g., the issue of periodicity itself).

INTEGRATED

The most comprehensive curricular conversations occur when students discover interrelationships across all of the elements in the curriculum, so that the parallel but independent discussions of an episodic curriculum begin to echo back on one another. As new elements enter into the conversation, they provide not only new contexts for exploring or redefining the established topic, but new perspectives on other elements in the conversation, and on the topic itself. Here, the conversation involves a process of continuing reconstrual not only of what has just been introduced, but, in light of new ideas, everything that has come before.

Integration of this sort occurs when the curriculum is made up of independent but interacting experiences. On the level of a unit, it can occur, for example, when students read case materials about an event in history, out of which they have to develop their own analyses and interpretations about what happened and why. In the language arts, it may occur as students contrast the voices of Native Americans with those of European colonists in exploring the literature of the colonial era, or read a cross-cultural collection of stories illuminating culturally different assumptions about the relationships among old age, wisdom, and respect. For a course as a whole, such integration occurs when the conversation continues across related units, allowing students to revisit earlier material in the light of new understandings. For sets of courses, it occurs when there are opportunities to consider them in relationship to one another, drawing out parallels and reflecting on discontinuities in order to generate a broader conversation than any one course may sustain.

Cecilia Rodrigues Milanés has described (1992) the advantages of such integration in a course at the University at Albany. She discusses her students' growing understanding of institutionalized racism in the United States while participating in a course that offered a much richer variety of texts than they were used to, including many by women, by African-American authors, and by Latin American authors. As Milanés described it, students' understanding of the issues "came, not suddenly, but as a result of dealing with the issue (and other related issues) over the semester: reading works treating it, writing about it, and talking about it with others" (p. 253). Though such a course must begin somewhere, books and ideas introduced early will be continually reconstrued as new ideas are encountered. As the course continues, participants will construct a shared representation of the curricular domain, and may very well redefine the topic with which they began. The knowledge they develop will be richly contextualized knowledge-in-action, developed through sustained conversation about related ideas.

An Example: An Integrated World Cultures Course

As an example of such integration, we can look at Emily French's World Cultures course (again drawn from my study of curriculum decision-making). Dr. French was chair of the English department at Riverhill High School and the driving force behind the department's push for the inclusion of more multicultural literature at all levels and grades—including the changes that Tony Harrison made in his Introduction to American Literature.

World Cultures was a ninth-grade correlated history and English course that students took for two periods back to back. Students were selected to represent the range of abilities at their school, based on middle-school teacher recommendations and middle-school grades. In addition, the class had an even balance of boys and girls, and an ethnic background that mirrored the school population.

The formal curriculum for this course was episodic, moving from one culture to another; but the course also fostered considerable integration across episodes. The course began with a month-long unit on "Perspectives" that established an initial frame, followed by six more units on broad regions, each of which might contain a variety of specific cultural groups: Native American, Middle Eastern, African, Japanese and Chinese, Indian, and European. The specific cultures within these broad regions changed from year to year.

French focused the course on patterns that could be used across cultures:

> We read folktales, dilemma tales, trickster tales, and
> orphan tales, and I give them patterns. They may
> not remember all the myths but they will remember
> the patterns and when they see [myths] later on the
> patterns will come up. . . . Then from all those
> myths of oral tradition I will then move into short
> stories, essays. From the myths and stories of one
> culture I go to the other cultures so they can see
> how the myths compare across cultures.

In each culture that the students studied—about one per
month—they began by analyzing these mythic patterns. Run-
ning concurrently with the proverbs and folktales were the
other genres she emphasized: novels, short stories, poetry.

Most important, the patterns for analyzing the tales became
a way for students to see patterns across the whole year's
course. Once they had been introduced to an orphan tale or a
trickster tale in one culture, they could begin to make compari-
sons when they encountered these patterns in the literature of
another culture. The patterns, then, became the focus of the
conversation; they were what French hoped the students
would carry away from the class.

Culture was studied through these literary patterns, each
unit addressing a different culture, using folktales, myths, and
other genres to evidence cultural values and perspectives. Although the course was structured around separate cultures,
the issue of multiculturalism was itself part of the conversation
French encouraged. She was constantly challenging students
to see the literature they were reading from beyond the perspective of their own culture and their own gender. For French
the topic of multiculturalism was at bottom a conversation
about the integrity of differences—cultural and individual.
Students talked about different ways of interpreting and responding to the literature they were reading. And they talked
about how the literature related to their individual lives.

There were many kinds of integration in this curriculum.
Writing was related to the reading. The literary patterns were
integrated with the cultural patterns; indeed, the students real-

ized the cultural patterns by articulating the literary patterns. The multicultural texts they read reflected the cultures they studied as well as the culture of their own classroom. Finally, this multicultural classroom stressed the differences inherent in literary interpretation and made that a topic of conversation as well.

Besides integrating within each unit, French also connected units, largely through the conversations about literary patterns that were discussed earlier. In each unit, she tried to address a new pattern, one that students could apply in retrospect to things they had already read, as well as to new texts. As she put it, she had to introduce these ideas "in pieces," or she would "have to spend so much time establishing the framework in the beginning I'd never get into the cultures." With such an approach to her curriculum, students' knowledge and understanding developed cumulatively throughout the year as they revisited important issues and concepts from new perspectives and with broader frames of reference. Like the students in Milanés's college course, they had the opportunity to develop richly contextualized knowledge-in-action as they used their developing understanding to explore new ideas and revisit old ones.

Integration in the sense discussed here goes much further than the kind of integration that is commonly advocated for language arts instruction. Integrated language arts usually refers to a curriculum in which the various types of language use (reading, writing, speaking, listening) and skill practice are related to one another, often by using thematic units that allow a range of activities to be related to the common theme. Integration at this level is a prerequisite for an integrated curricular conversation, but it is not sufficient. True integration requires real grounds for conversation and reconstrual as the curriculum evolves. Many thematic units are too shallow for such reconstrual, no matter how carefully the various language arts are integrated into them (for a critique, see Lipson, Valencia, Wixson, and Peters 1993; for guidance on how to avoid such problems, see Walmsley 1994). The result is that while language activities may all emphasize a common topic, the activities are not drawn from a coherent conversational domain.

CONSTRUCTING CURRICULAR DOMAINS

The examples of curriculum discussed in this chapter come from a study of how accomplished teachers create a coherent curriculum within their individual courses: What do they do that gives them and their students a sense of direction and continuity? Some of the lessons that can be drawn from their experiences have already been discussed: The need for relatedness among experiences, for materials of high quality, and for sufficient material to sustain conversation but not so much material as to overwhelm it.

The discussion of the different structures that are used to organize curricula suggests other important features to consider in constructing domains for conversation. Curricula of the type I have been calling "integrated" provide the most structural support for sustained conversation. In classes with an integrated curriculum, students as well as the teacher are more likely to develop a sense of where the conversation is going, of what is interesting and what related. They learn in a very real sense to carry on the conversation on their own. They can continue it when the teacher is not present, and they can help new students "catch on" to what is important, rather than "catch up" by recapitulating everything that has gone before. They also come to see their subject as an ongoing discourse, one in which important issues can be revisited, and earlier experiences can be reinterpreted in light of new learning. Thus the knowledge they gain is dynamic rather than static; in the terms of the present book, it is knowledge-in-action rather than knowledge-out-of-context. It changes as the result of their own continuing explorations, as well as from hearing new voices enter into the conversations. Such new voices might be those of their classmates or teacher, or they might be voices from the broader traditions of conversation within which their classroom discussions are situated. "Great works'' from many cultures and many ages have their place in these conversations because they have something to offer, not because someone outside of the conversation has deemed them important.

The other structures that I have discussed in this chapter also have a role, however, and come into play when the task of integration seems more than the teacher or curriculum planner can manage. Catalogs and collections, for example, provide a way to think about how some of the otherwise unrelated parts of English studies get handled within a single course; in the classrooms from which I have drawn examples of the literature curriculum, separate strands of vocabulary and language study, and sometimes of writing, existed alongside the conversational domain for literature. Episodic curricula, on the other hand, provide starting points in exploring domains where the overarching ideas are not clear, or where the size of the domain is so large that the task of integration seems initially overwhelming. In an episodic curriculum, individual episodes may be well integrated even if the curriculum as a whole is not. Rather than seeing this as a limitation or failure, we should recognize how unusual complete integration is, in our lives or in our teaching; the perspective that it requires is large, and the demands it makes on us are not trivial.

Many of the issues that arise in planning the curriculum of an individual course surface in a different form when one is thinking about relationships among courses. American high schools have been criticized for offering a ''shopping mall'' curriculum, essentially a catalog of options with little thought to their relationships and relative value (Powell, Farrar, and Cohen 1985). The critique is just as applicable at the college level, and generally leads toward proposals for a more integrated and less elective educational experience. Many different issues get tangled in such discussions, however: They mix issues of the relative value of different topics, the promise of interdisciplinary approaches, and the value of shared experiences amid the impersonal structure of large institutions. From the perspective adopted here, we need to think about the kinds of conversations that will engage students, and the relationships among those conversations. It seems misguided to expect that an entire educational experience can be encompassed within one grand conversation—there are after all many different traditions of discourse that are valued in our culture, and a variety of intellectual tools that we would hope students would master. On the other hand, there are real relationships among many of the separate conversations that now form the curriculum, and finding ways to examine their commonalities and differences can only be enriching.

In helping students enter into curricular domains, finding an initial topic or direction for conversation is critical. How this can best be done is less obvious. From the examples we have studied, it seems that the most successful topics could be expressed as broad questions that invite discussion and debate across a broad domain of experiences. Tony Harrison, introduced in chapter 4, phrased the new topic for his American Literature course as "Who chooses the canon?" and the subsequent evolution of the conversation in his class could be construed as a progressive exploration of that question. Emily French never posed a similar question for her World Cultures class, but we could construe her curriculum as an extended conversation around something like "What does it mean to be human in a multicultural world?"

Questions are easily trivialized, however. They can be given right answers (Huckleberry Finn *was* a good boy) or used with curriculum materials that won't support real conversation. The liberal educationists also began with a set of questions or "great issues": "What is our destiny? What is a good life? How can we achieve a good society?" (Hutchins 1952, p. 56), but in tracing these through their library of Great Books of the Western World they reduced them to 102 alphabetically organized "basic ideas" and 2,987 related topics (e.g., "angel, animal, aristocracy, art, . . . , habit, happiness, history, . . . , science, sense, sin"; Adler 1952).

At best, a formal curriculum can provide an overview of experiences and topics for conversation that meet the criteria of relatedness, quality, and quantity, and that suggest a domain that is integrated rather than fragmented. The enacted curriculum—that which takes place in the classroom—will always rely on the negotiations that take place among the participants—teachers and students—to determine what will be interesting and important to explore within a given tradition for a particular class at a particular point in time. In turn, the received curriculum—the knowledge-in-action the students take from it—will depend on how successfully that negotiation engages the attention and builds upon the prior understandings of each individual.

Recent Curriculum
Proposals as Domains
for Conversation

The past few years have seen a reawakening of interest in issues of curriculum, after several decades in which ideas about curriculum were little discussed. In this chapter, I want to explore the strengths and weaknesses of some of the more influential of the discussions and proposals that have attempted to deal with the English language arts, and also to look at one historical statement, *An Experience Curriculum in English* (Hatfield 1935), that represented the most extensive attempt to exemplify a language arts curriculum of knowledge-in-action during the Progressive Era. Even today, this volume continues to be cited as a successful attempt to articulate a student-centered curriculum. Considering these statements will illustrate both the current state of discussion of the English language arts curriculum and the kinds of questions that viewing curriculum as culturally significant domains for conversation leads us to ask.

I will begin with *An Experience Curriculum in English* and move from there to E. D. Hirsch's proposals for cultural literacy, recent attempts by the National Council of Teachers of English and related organizations to redefine the breadth of English instruction, and the twelfth-grade Pacesetter English course under development by the College Board and the National Council.

AN EXPERIENCE CURRICULUM IN ENGLISH

In 1929, faced with an array of proposals for making the teaching of English more student-centered and experience-oriented, the National Council of Teachers of English established a curriculum commission charged with developing a "pattern cur-riculum" that would provide a stable reference point (on the report and its context, see Applebee 1974). Believing that the attempt to specify a single curriculum for as diverse a country as the United States would be "folly" (Hatfield 1935, p. v), they sought instead to provide a model that could be reworked and elaborated in each local community. As its title suggests, the volume produced by the curriculum commission (chaired by the Council's executive secretary, Wilbur Hatfield) em-braced the metaphor of English as experience: "Experience is the best of all schools. . . . *The ideal curriculum consists of well-selected experiences*" (p. 3; emphasis in original). The concern with experience that dominated the report derives from John Dewey (1899, 1916) and the progressive educators who elaborated on him, and is an early manifestation of em-phasis on knowledge-in-action. (Dewey is not, however, cited in the report itself.) Through well-selected experiences, the argument went, students would acquire the knowledge and skills they needed. The concept of experience that structured the report was quite shallow, however; the role of English was "to provide the communication (speaking, writing, listening, reading) necessary to the conduct of social activities, and to provide indirect (or vicarious) experiences where direct expe-riences are impossible or undesirable" (p. 4). Given this ver-sion of the role of English, virtually any activity could be treated as a "language experience," and virtually every activ-ity was.

In order to determine what should be included in the curricu-lum, the commission turned to the procedures that Bobbitt had outlined earlier (1918, 1924): They sought to "survey life, noting the experiences most people have," as well as "the desirable possible experiences they miss" (p. 3). The effect of this process was to fragment natural domains of activity, as the commission struggled to ensure that all of the "needs" of adult life would find a place in the curriculum. Instead of experiences that reflected traditions of knowing and doing, the "experience strands" that were used to organize the curricu-lum reflected traditional views of the English language arts as made up of a variety of different language skills. They included "experiences" in literature, reading, creative expression, speech, writing, and instrumental grammar, as well as corrective teaching and electives. How far these strayed from the ideal of experiences that embodied real purposes and integrated the practical and the theoretical is apparent in the Writing Experience strands for the elementary grades. These included, among others, Strand A, Social Letters; Strand B, Business Letters; and Strand C, Blank Forms (pp. 185–91). The commission believed strongly that language skills could be effectively developed only in the context of language use, yet the language activities that they went on to propose were themselves stripped of the social, cultural, and disciplinary traditions that might have given them meaning and vitality. Rather than sustaining conversational action within culturally significant domains, the units tended to trivialize the subject matter. Even literature became a body of information, or sometimes "vicarious" experience, that might better be gained in other ways.

Thus the final unit in a strand of literature experiences for the elementary school, titled "Exploring the Social World," had as its primary objective "to enjoy simple books about trains, ships, airplanes, radio et cetera." It had as a supporting objective "to recognize the unusual and therefore interesting features of each mode of travel. To see some of the practical as well as the picturesque phases of transportation" (p. 35). In the secondary school, a unit from the same strand had as its primary objective "to observe man's industrial expansion." The supporting objectives were "to compare industry as it was before our time with our own industrial age; to participate vicariously with men and women who worked and are working under conditions both good and bad; to analyze our present economic system, and to compare it with systems of other days" (p. 49). Suggested readings for this unit included, among others, *Silas Marner, The Last of the Mohicans,* and *Two Years Before the Mast.* Given the focus of the unit, these books were to be read for whatever information they might yield about economics and working conditions in previous eras, rather than as part of a conversation that treated them as literature, with their own unique contribution to make to human understanding (Langer 1995).

We can see three immediate problems in the approach to curriculum developed by the curriculum commission. The first was the definition of the subject area in terms of an inventory of individual needs. This immediately fragmented the experiences that were to be offered and removed them from larger domains of discourse from which they might have gained meaning and significance. The second, and related, problem was the lack of any inherent connectedness among the experiences, so that in spite of the organization into strands, each experience would proceed in essential isolation from the others. (The units in each strand were meant to last anywhere from five to fifteen days, but the report noted that these did not need to be consecutive; in fact the "unit" could be spread out over the whole year [p. iv].) As a result, the curriculum provided no way for real conversation to develop. The third problem was a loss of any sense of the uniqueness of English as a subject area. Many of the experiences that were singled out could just as comfortably be embedded in social studies or science curricula. Indeed, given the definition of English as communication and vicarious experience, that is arguably where many of the experiences belonged.[1] Seeking to define a curriculum that would be, in their words, embedded in "pupils' dynamic experiences of work and play, of joy and sorrow" (p. 14), the commission lacked a sense of how to untangle the conversations that were unique to the field of English studies from those pre-, inter-, or cross-disciplinary conversations to which the English language arts might usefully contribute. Rather than a useful cross-fertilization of ideas, the result

1. The commission was ambivalent on this point. A subcommittee produced a second report, *A Correlated Curriculum* (Weeks 1936), which approached correlation with other subjects cautiously, as an experiment that was worth trying but as yet unproven. Eventually the movement toward integration of subject areas was rejected by English teachers who found the values of their own subject being overwhelmed by those of the correlated subjects. See Applebee 1974.

was a loss of focus and coherence, and a reversion to units on filling out blank forms, or learning about the economic system by reading *The Last of the Mohicans*.

CULTURAL LITERACY

I want to move now from historical statements to curriculum proposals that are taken seriously in schools today. Of these, the one that has most captured the popular imagination, if not that of the education profession, has been E. D. Hirsch's proposals for a curriculum devoted to the development of cultural literacy (Hirsch 1987; Hirsch, Kett, and Trefil 1988).

Hirsch grounds his proposals in recent studies of reading comprehension, which have demonstrated the important role that background knowledge plays in student understanding. Without appropriate background knowledge, even simple texts can be difficult or impossible to understand; with appropriate background knowledge, the meaning of "difficult" texts can become quite apparent. Hirsch's argument moves rapidly from laboratory studies of text comprehension to the knowledge necessary for effective participation in society at large. Full membership in American society—including the ability to share in its opportunities for equality and advancement—depends on having the cultural knowledge that underlies public discourse. Without appropriate knowledge of the dominant tradition, people will be doomed to misunderstand and to be misunderstood.

Examining the school curriculum and student achievement, Hirsch concludes that American schools are sadly lacking in their ability to develop the necessary shared background knowledge. He proposes that schools adopt a curriculum of cultural literacy, systematically introducing students across the grades to essential cultural reference points drawn from history, literature, science, the arts, and popular culture. Many of the elements of cultural literacy were listed in an appendix to his original volume, and in expanded form in a later *Dictionary of Cultural Literacy* (Hirsch, Kett, and Trefil 1988).

Hirsch's goal is clearly to enable all students to enter into culturally significant traditions of discourse. His social and moral purposes are reflected in his rhetoric. By engaging with him in his project to promote cultural literacy, we will be

> breaking the cycle of illiteracy for deprived children; raising the living standard of families who have been illiterate; making our country more competitive in international markets; achieving greater social justice; enabling all citizens to participate in the political process; bringing us closer to the Ciceronian ideal of universal public discourse—in short, achieving fundamental goals of the Founders at the birth of the republic. (P. 145)

There are two problems in Hirsch's curriculum proposals. The first stems from the singleness of the vision of shared cultural literacy, and the narrowness of the tradition into which students are being asked to enter. Hirsch's tradition of public discourse is essentially the Arnoldian tradition discussed in chapter 3, the "great conversation" of the Western world as it was conceptualized by American liberal educationists in the early part of the twentieth century. Particularly in his initial lists, as many commentators have pointed out, Hirsch showed little awareness of the accomplishments of women, of people of color, or of anyone outside the Western heritage highlighted in his reference to Cicero in the section quoted above.

Others could broaden Hirsch's proposals, however, if they represented a helpful way to think about the educational task. In fact, they do not. Although Hirsch's argument for the importance of cultural literacy is grounded in an influential series of recent cognitive studies of reading comprehension and interpretation, his pedagogy is surprisingly limited and ignores other findings from the same body of research. The work on reading comprehension that he cites is primarily concerned with demonstrating the embedded nature of knowledge—the extent to which what we know is embedded in structures of knowing and doing rather than easily available, or readily use-

ful, as knowledge-out-of-context.[2] Yet oddly, Hirsch's proposals for curriculum downplay this aspect of the work on which
his argument is based. He proposes instead that by exposing
students to systematic lists of culturally important information, they will gain the background knowledge they need to
attain the broad goals he has outlined. But as I suggested in
earlier chapters, such catalogs of information frustrate rather
than encourage conversational action. Instead of helping students enter into significant traditions of discourse, his pedagogy seems destined to shut them out.

Hirsch's arguments have been vilified by many professional
educators, as much for the political implications of the tradition he emphasizes as for the characteristics of his pedagogy.
His arguments have had a salutary effect on discussions of
curriculum, however, in reminding us that what we teach does
matter. Whether we accept the particular content he singles
out for attention, we cannot easily argue that the substance of
the curriculum is irrelevant to the knowledge we want students
to develop. Surprisingly, before Hirsch's book, there was a
tendency to do so.

THE ENGLISH COALITION

At about the same time that Hirsch's proposals were getting
widespread attention, the National Council of Teachers of English, the Modern Language Association, and a coalition of
other organizations interested in the teaching of English con-
vened a month-long conference to reconsider goals and approaches in English teaching at all levels. Meeting in the sum-
mer of 1987, they summarized their deliberations in two
volumes, one a compilation of writings produced at the conference, edited by Richard Lloyd-Jones and Andrea Lunsford
(1989), and the other written after the conference by Peter
Elbow (1990).

In contrast to Hirsch's attempt to define at least a part of

2. For a readable summary of the work and its implications, targeted at a
public rather than a technical audience, see *Becoming a Nation of Readers*
(Anderson, Hiebert, Scott, and Wilkinson 1984).

English through its content,[3] the coalition conference moved to define it through its pedagogy. Echoing *An Experience Curriculum in English,* the coalition sought coherence through an emphasis on what they called "practicing" in English. By "practicing"—an awkward term that has been largely ignored by the profession at large—they meant the language experiences and language activities in which students would engage, and through which they would gain new skills and competencies. "Practicing" seems to have represented a compromise between the "praxis" of critical theory and the more pragmatic "activities" or "experiences" of the classroom. It also provided a way to incorporate the emphasis on process-oriented instruction that developed in all areas of the language arts during the 1970s and 1980s, and that had in particular become the dominant ideology in the teaching of writing by the time of the coalition conference. (On the development of process pedagogies, see Applebee 1986; Applebee and Purves 1992; Hillocks 1986.)

The conference had no use for formal curricula, or for lists of content such as Hirsch's. In order to share its vision of effective teaching and learning, the coalition relied on "illustrations" of effective practice. The illustrations were offered in the belief that effective teaching and learning could be instantiated in many different ways in response to the unique circumstances of local schools and communities. By examining examples of good practice, teachers would be able to develop their own curricula based on similar principles.

The approach taken by the coalition was in large part a reaction to the prescriptive nature of Hirsch's lists and to the atomization of the curriculum that could result from lists of any sort. The result, however, was that the coalition declined to provide any firm guidelines for the English language arts curriculum. Broad rationales for instruction were developed by separate subgroups representing elementary, secondary, and college teaching, but these statements offered platitudes

---

3. Hirsch never claimed that his curriculum for cultural literacy should replace the curriculum in English or any other subject.

about the importance of language learning rather than helpful guidance about how instruction might be organized and carried out. Like the curriculum commission before it, the coalition conference developed a vision of experiences with language without a vision of the traditions within which those experiences might take place. There was no sense of a domain for conversational action, or even that one was needed.

Instead, the coalition discussed the English language arts in terms of language practices and processes. There was no clear conceptualization of the universe of study, whether in terms of skills or in terms of significant traditions of discourse. For my purposes, the most interesting point is the difficulties that arose out of a lack of a shared language to talk about curriculum issues. In a sense, the discussions at the coalition conference attempted to define English studies as a pedagogy for language learning, ducking the issue of curriculum altogether. Within the relatively homogeneous community of the coalition conference, this strategy allowed discussion to continue. As an approach to articulating a more public vision of English studies, however, the approach through pedagogy alone collapses. Even within the community of conference participants, the consensus that seemed to have been reached quickly began to disintegrate. Peter Elbow, for example, in his report on the conference (1990), devoted much of his book to a retrospective commentary on issues that the coalition conference had avoided—and even offered a modest proposal for a list of common readings, changing each year, as an appendix to his argument.

PACESETTER ENGLISH

More recently, another project, cosponsored by the College Board and the National Council of Teachers of English, has sought to develop a new twelfth-grade English curriculum. Conceived of as part of the national effort to reform instruction, the Pacesetter projects sought to develop a more rigorous, thoughtful curriculum for all students in key subject areas. (Initial development efforts focused on English, mathematics, science, world history, and Spanish.) By concentrating on the twelfth grade as a "capstone" of the secondary school curriculum, the organizers hoped to have a "trickle down" effect on earlier years of schooling as well. Coordinated by the College Board, the Pacesetter projects drew on the Board's previous experiences in designing and implementing Advanced Placement courses. By concentrating on "capstone" twelfth-grade courses, the Board hoped to have the same effects on the rest of the curriculum that the Advanced Placement program had had. Unlike Advanced Placement, however, the Pacesetter program was conceived and presented as a set of courses appropriate for students of all levels of experience and ability rather than for an academic elite.

Many members of the English Pacesetter advisory board also participated in the English coalition conference, but Pacesetter involved a much smaller group and had a more limited and specific task. Its success or failure will be determined by the degree to which teachers and their school boards adopt the resulting program of curriculum and assessment.

The rationale for Pacesetter English drew on a variety of current discussions of the nature of English studies. Early overview documents cite, in particular, Robert Scholes's work on textual power (1985), recent work in feminist and multicultural studies, and early drafts of my discussions of curriculum as a culturally significant domain for conversation. The course is thus a partial application of the concept of curriculum as a domain for conversation in the practical process of curriculum development. The Pacesetter planning meetings took place as my ideas about curricular conversations were developing out of a series of studies of curriculum decision-making (Applebee 1993a; Applebee, Burroughs, and Stevens 1994); the discussions in the Pacesetter committee influenced my formulation as well as being influenced by it.[4] Pacesetter is not, however,

---

4. The Pacesetter background documents, capturing and extending the discussions of the advisory board, were drafted by Dennie Palmer Wolf. Short published versions of the rationale are available in Wolf 1995 and Scholes 1995. For an early critique and response, see Daniels 1994 and Elias 1994. Holtzman (1995) offers another committee member's view of the conflicts and compromises inherent in the development process.

a "critical test" of those ideas: Rather it is the first effort at curriculum construction in which those ideas played any part.

The Pacesetter project embodied both a curriculum and a pedagogy. The pedagogy reflected the conventional wisdom that had been embodied in the coalition conference. English studies were to involve students in explorations of significant issues, in which knowledge and skills would develop in the context of use. Teachers were seen as facilitators, prompters, or guides rather than as providers of knowledge. Assessment was to be ongoing and embedded in the process of teaching and learning rather than separated into artificial assessment episodes. The rhetoric of a student-centered, constructivist pedagogy flows through the Pacesetter documents: portfolios, collaborative learning, thoughtfulness, empowerment, integration. In the terminology of the present book, such discussions were concerned with the manner of instruction; in particular, the project sought to ensure that teaching and learning would be designed to help students enter into significant domains of conversation.

Like the English coalition conference, the English Pacesetter committee was also reluctant to prescribe a single universal curriculum for all students. Instead, following a model already well institutionalized in the Advanced Placement program, they sought to develop a broad framework with illustrative units that teachers could use as a starting point but that they could also replace with materials of their own (Wolf 1995). The notion of curriculum as conversation was echoed in the course title, Voices of Modern Cultures, and in activities meant to draw students into debates about the texts and issues that structure the course. The course has certain key features that could be instantiated in many different ways, depending on the classroom context and the resources available, but that would preserve the distinctive characteristics of the curriculum even as its details varied. These key features included use of a combination of older works that may or may not be new to the curriculum (e.g., *Othello, Their Eyes Were Watching God*) and more contemporary works to illustrate important conversational domains; integration of reading, writing, and oral language across activities based on a variety of media; collaborative and small-group activities; emphasis on extended explorations of significant topics rather than one-shot activities; embedded assessment of student learning; and opportunities for students to engage in independent projects. As a set, these features were intended to ensure that the curriculum would stress knowledge-in-action rather than knowledge-out-of-context.

Pacesetter English was also designed to be evolving rather than static. The pilot version consisted of a series of seven units conceived of as helping students enter into culturally significant conversations about how language is used to create ourselves and others, and how we preserve and renew the traditions we inherit even as new traditions emerge. The conversations were closely tied to Scholes's (1985) goals of developing textual power in a wide range of genres and media—to read closely and respond thoughtfully, as well as to generate original work appropriate to a wide range of tasks and audiences. In their explorations, students would both consolidate what they had learned across twelve years of schooling, and look forward to their new life after school. (Disagreements about the particular content of the course seem likely to continue forever; I myself wonder whether the emphasis on uses of language, rather than on human experience in its depth and complexity, is overly specialized and inherently unengaging.)

In the course, students move from an examination of how they are situated as individuals who are insiders in some groups and outsiders in others to an examination of the experience of "being the other" (Scholes 1995). They are invited to explore the cultures and voices in a single complex text (illustrated in the pilot materials by *Their Eyes Were Watching God*), to examine a text from the past (*Othello*) in its historical context and as a voice in contemporary conversations, to engage in extended study of film as an example of new languages within a culture (*The Man Who Shot Liberty Valance*), to revisit an event or period of cultural significance as the site for considering how cultural conversations are mediated through the media (journalism, film, and videos from the sixties), and to reflect on the issues and texts they have been reading throughout the year.[5] In each unit, students explore a range of related and contrasting voices, and learn to add their own voices to the conversation in a variety of genres and media. The units are linked, so that early units introduce issues that will be dealt with more thoroughly later, and later units reconnect to earlier activities. The course is thus designed to be "integrated" in the sense I discussed in chapter 6.

Assessment poses special problems for the Pacesetter program. On the one hand, there is a commitment to assessments that are integrated into the ongoing curriculum and consistent with its goals and practices rather than the standardized, decontextualized tests that are typically used to enhance reliability and comparability. On the other hand, there is a commitment to public reporting of progress and to accountability across different Pacesetter sites. This set of goals is relatively easy to achieve in the individual classroom through assessments based on ongoing activities gathered together into portfolios of student work. Finding ways to compare this work across classrooms that may differ in the selections that are read and the assignments that are given is much more difficult. (It also immediately raises the level of mistrust about the intentions of the College Board and its contractor, Educational Testing Service: A number of commentators see these institutions as revenue-driven and harmful to the educational enterprise; e.g., Vopat 1995.) Although the Pacesetter committees in all subject areas have struggled with this problem, it remains one of the major issues raised by a national commission established by the College Board itself to review Pacesetter in the

---

5. The pilot versions of the units were titled as follows: 1. Introduction to Voices of Modern Cultures; 2. Stranger in the Village: Encountering the Other, Being the Other; 3. Culture as a Medley of Voices: Permitting New Voices to Enter; 4. Renewing Old Voices: Producing and Reviewing Dramatic Work; 5. New Languages in a Culture: The Case of Film; 6. Recollections and Representations: The Ways in Which Cultural Conversations/Conflicts Are Mediated through the Media; 7. Considering the Changing Voice, the Changing Village (returning to issues of language in the context of transformation, and reviewing their own language learning through the course). See Scholes 1995.

context of national efforts at educational reform (Castor and Reynolds 1994). While praising the attempt to integrate assessment with ongoing instruction, the commission went on to say that Pacesetter development needed to give still more attention to the relationships between instructional and accountability versions of assessment, as well as to reporting formats that would allow results to be useful both for instruction and accountability (pp. 19–21). If Pacesetter is to achieve its goals, these issues have to be resolved in ways that keep the emphasis on the knowledge-in-action that students will gain as they learn to enter into the conversations around which the course is organized, rather than on the knowledge-out-of-context that is more easily tested and compared across sites.

The Pacesetter English curriculum is still a work in progress. During the 1994–95 academic year, it was piloted by some eighty-five teachers in fifty-four schools in fifteen states. The initial materials will continue to evolve as a result of their experiences, and as larger groups of teachers become involved and begin to shape it to reflect their own needs. In its present form, Voices of Modern Cultures represents a radical departure in overt content from the typical twelfth-grade course, which tends to focus either on British literature or on electives of the students' own choosing (Applebee 1993b). The suggested texts, however, are familiar, and in and of themselves will not significantly alter students' experiences. This will require a shift in the topics of conversation around the texts, and in the degree to which students are invited to enter into those conversations rather than merely to observe them. The Pacesetter committee clearly intended for those changes to take place, but successful implementation will require new ways of thinking about the issues these texts raise—the conversations in which they participate—as well as changes in approaches to teaching and testing. Only time will tell whether teachers are ready for such shifts, or whether curriculum and assessment will be redefined in more traditional terms as the development process reaches out to more school districts and larger groups of teachers.

CONVERSATIONS THAT MATTER

The Pacesetter course, while representing a significant rethinking of the senior year, is silent about the rest of the curriculum. The principles that shaped its initial versions, however, would imply a major rethinking of curriculum at other grade levels as well. Some of that rethinking is already under way, evident for example in recent reexaminations of thematic teaching in the elementary school (Lipson, Valencia, Wixson, and Peters 1993; Walmsley 1994), and in proposals such as Graff's (1992) for ways to provide more conversation across courses in colleges and universities. These proposals share a concern with creating more integrated contexts in which students can learn to enter into curricular conversations of substance and depth.

What we still lack is a successful parsing of the many possible domains for conversation in ways that ensure some sort of reasonable range and variety across the grades. Walmsley (1994) notes that the specific topics students study are less important than the broader conversations in which they engage:

> For example, it really doesn't matter if children
> study whales or penguins or sharks because studying
> any animal in any depth will bring to the surface
> knowledge about animals' roles in nature, their rela-
> tionship to humans, and our responsibilities to them.
> (P. xvii)

Unfortunately, as the present chapter has suggested, we have in the past made more attempts to specify elaborate lists of specific topics than we have to explicate the underlying conversations.

The specific topics for study may ultimately be best determined by the individual teacher or school, as Walmsley's comment implies. It simply does not matter if twelfth graders in one school read *Othello* and those in another read *King Lear,* and it does not even really matter if twelfth graders read Shakespeare at all. (In the curriculum as it exists at present, most don't.) But teachers do need a better sense than we have at present of the things that are worth talking about across the grades—the conversations that matter within and across the major school subjects. And they need more materials that attempt to reorganize the curriculum so that it is easier to undertake thought-provoking conversations that provide students with opportunities to learn the structure and content of domains that matter, as well as the interrelationships among them.

EIGHT

Toward a Pedagogy
of Knowledge-in-Action

The close links between what and how we teach have already been noted in previous chapters. If teaching and learning are not orchestrated to facilitate students' entry into the domains for conversation that constitute a curriculum, we will have changed the labels but not the substance of education. In this chapter I want to bring together a variety of perspectives on instruction within the general framework that I have been discussing.

ENTERING DOMAINS

The classroom represents an intersection of many systems of discourse competing for the students' attention. These include the expectations of the home, the public culture of the community and nation, the pressures of peer culture, and the desire for individual attention and differentiation from and within the group. Classroom discussion and literacy events will be shaped by all of these discourses, not just by that of the academic tradition. And the teacher's ability to mediate among these traditions, drawing from them rather than fighting against them, will have a substantial impact on the learning that occurs.

For the most part, this mediation occurs tacitly, with neither teacher nor student aware that it is happening. Instead it occurs as part of the background of expectations that are created within the classroom, expectations that are *both* characteristic of the classroom *and* embodiments of broader traditions of discourse. An essential part of these expectations has to do with understanding the conventions of conversation within a particular domain: what is talked about, how, and why. Entering into a tradition of discourse involves accepting its purposes, its general topic or direction (Grice 1975). These purposes both motivate individual discourse and determine which contributions will be interesting, relevant, and effective. (Thus the purposes of scientific discourse validate one set of conversations as relevant and interesting, while those of literary discourse validate another.) Purposes within a domain, like the domain itself, are socially constructed; in "accepting" the general topic or direction of conversation, an individual is learning how to take appropriate action. And like all social constructs, these purposes will change with time and with the people who are participating.

Ann Haas Dyson, studying young children's experiences with school, has pointed out (1993, 1994) that classroom discourse reflects many different purposes, only some of which are academic. A student's contribution (oral or written) may reflect her purposes of social cohesion and social manipulation as much as artful performance and sharing of information. Part of the essential role of the teacher is in navigating among the many interacting purposes that shape classroom discourse, helping students reconstrue their own contributions so that they fall within the relevant academic domain.

Failing to acknowledge the many different purposes that shape students' talking and writing can frustrate teaching and learning. When eight-year-old Ayesha has entertained her classmates with a catalog of favorite rap singers, asking her to revise and elaborate her "report" is likely to strike her as irrelevant (Dyson 1993, 1994). In mediating among discourses, a teacher must recognize the complex motivations behind students' contributions, rather than ignoring those that are not clearly academic.

Even within an academic domain, the expectations that govern classroom discourse operate at many different levels. They reflect social and cultural practices that are realized through differing rhetorical strategies, genre structures, stylistic preferences, vocabulary, and role relationships. Very few of these are likely to be articulated directly by teachers or students.

Instead, they emerge out of subtly signaled judgments of the effectiveness and relevance of students' contributions to the daily discourse of the classroom: what is elaborated, what is rejected, and what is ignored. Even expectations that are explicitly signaled by teachers are likely to be so contextually embedded as to be meaningless out of context. Thus teachers in subjects as different as biology, history, and literature are likely to ask students to "provide evidence," "analyze," and "elaborate" in the course of talk and writing. But the very real differences in the meaning of those terms from subject to subject are rarely if ever explained. Most of us, in fact, cannot explain the differences, because they are tacit, embodied in our knowledge-in-action but never overtly or explicitly defined (see Langer 1992).

Though such differences may rarely be the overt topic of instruction, students nevertheless learn the characteristic discourse of each subject through the mediation of the teacher's actions. In each classroom, they learn what counts as interesting and appropriate, what can be said and how to say it. In literature, for example, students' independent responses to texts quite quickly begin to conform to the critical perspectives in which their teachers have been trained. If teachers take a New Critical approach, so will their students; if teachers stress historical perspectives and cultural contexts, their students will too (Applebee 1977). The differences among such perspectives can be quite profound: They include criteria for evaluation, types of evidence offered in support of opinions, and the intertextual field of references that are considered most relevant. Such effects extend even to regional and national preferences in response (Purves 1973): Nations differ in their literary and critical traditions, and these differences exert powerful and predictable influences on what students learn.

The operation and importance of these systems of tacit expectations imply that teachers themselves must be active participants in the disciplines they teach, not only as undergraduates in their initial training but on a lifelong basis. This is a precondition if they are in turn to help students enter into traditions of discourse that are living today, rather than traditions that encapsulate the issues and arguments of the past. A generalist background will give teachers a passing knowledge of many subjects, but it will not give them the depth of tacit knowledge they need to mediate effectively between the classroom and the broader traditions of their subject.

This can be particularly problematic in the teaching of school subjects that incorporate a number of different disciplines, such as social studies and the sciences, and to some extent English. For a teacher in training, this creates a classic tension between breadth and depth of study—to know one subject well or many subjects poorly. The tacit knowledge needed to mediate effectively between the discourses of the classroom and those of the academic tradition, however, is likely to develop only through depth of study. Teachers of these subjects are likely to be more effective if they are well trained in one of the related disciplines than if they have experienced only a general introduction to all of them. Although most of their own explorations of disciplinary traditions will be inappropriate in their school classrooms, such explorations help teachers develop the tacit knowledge, the knowledge-in-action, necessary to mediate between those traditions and the classroom. It is that knowledge of how to converse effectively within the tradition that will allow them in turn to help their own students enter into the domain. Thus I am arguing against proposals to align the subject-matter training of teachers more closely to the school curriculum, and in favor of proposals that insist that secondary school teachers complete a full-scale major in a subject they will teach; this is the best way to develop their own knowledge-in-action, and to ensure their own comfort in participating in conversations that matter.

Knowledge of the academic tradition is only one half of what teaching requires, however. Lee Shulman (1987) has used the term *pedagogical content knowledge* to describe teachers' knowledge of how the tradition must be transformed for use in the classroom. Shulman argues that this is quite distinct from the disciplinary knowledge that teachers also need to develop. Pedagogical content knowledge includes an understanding of what students are learning as they learn a new

subject, how activities can be structured to support such learning, and how curricular conversations can be established and
maintained in the complex social world of the classroom. In
the teaching of literature, for example, pedagogical content
knowledge includes an understanding of the strategies readers
use in developing their envisionments of what they are reading
(Langer 1990, 1995), and of how instruction can be planned to
encourage rather than thwart the development of those strategies. Pedagogical content knowledge is essential in helping students enter into significant domains for conversation, but does
not arise directly out of a teacher's own experience in the
disciplinary tradition.

A considerable part of teachers' tacit knowledge of the academic tradition and of pedagogy is expressed in the conventions they establish for discourse within their classrooms. In
my studies of the ways curriculum emerges over time in individual classrooms, the presence of such a set of tacit conventions of discourse has been one of the most consistent features
of accomplished teaching and learning (Applebee, Burroughs,
and Stevens 1994). These conventions provide the essential
backdrop against which everything else takes place. Conventions for discussion govern aspects of both the form and content of discussion and interaction. They determine, on the one
hand, how discussion is to be organized in exploring the domain (ranging from teacher-led, whole-class activities to cooperative learning groups to individual seatwork), and on the
other, what topics and issues are considered appropriate as
part of the English language arts in general and literature in
particular (ranging from textual analysis to issues in contemporary life). In a sense, the discussion conventions govern and
determine those things that stay the same even as a class progresses: how discussion takes place, what is talked about, and
where the discussion is expected to lead.

Discussion conventions are a significant part of what students are learning: They are a tacit statement of what it means
to "do English" or "do math." In many cases students learn
the conventions governing discussion of the domain quickly,
and act accordingly, changing the nature of their participation

as they move from one school classroom to another. Studying college and graduate school courses, however, a number of researchers (Berkenkotter, Huckin, and Ackerman 1988, Herrington 1985, and McCarthy 1987) have shown the difficulties that students can experience when they encounter domains with conventions that differ too much from what they have come to expect in previous classes. Lisa Delpit (1986, 1988) and Victor Villanueva (1993), discussing the problems of minority students at risk of school failure, have made similar points about the importance of learning "the rules of the game"—which are quite different from the overtly presented curriculum. Learning the conventions of discussion of each classroom and subject can be a long and stressful process. Not all students succeed.

MEDIATING THE TRADITION

Discussion conventions usually operate tacitly, though they are subject to study and change. Much of the current effort at instructional reform has in fact focused on conventions of discussion: Teachers have been urged to ask more open-ended and higher-order questions, to encourage small-group discussion and collaborative activities, and to value students' questions and tentative formulations rather than concentrating on final products. Such changes in patterns of instruction are designed to shift the emphasis from knowledge-out-of-context toward knowledge-in-action, and thus toward students' abilities to enter as active participants in the conversational domain.

Traditions of discourse can be quite complicated, however, and accomplished participation may result only from lengthy study and experience within the domain. It is not enough simply to invite students to enter: Effective teaching requires active as well as tacit mediation between the complex social structure of the classroom and the academic tradition.

Mihaly Csikszentmihalyi has studied the factors that help students enter into a variety of culturally significant domains for conversation, including art, music, science, mathematics, and athletics. Focusing on the high school experiences of talented youth, Csikszentmihalyi argues that the most effective learning environments involve a productive tension between support and challenge, allowing students to have the pleasure of mastery as well as the challenge of moving beyond their present accomplishments (Csikszentmihalyi, Rathunde, and Whalen 1993). The characteristics he describes are very similar to those that Judith Langer and I have found in our studies of how teachers establish and maintain challenging environments for teaching and learning (Applebee 1984; Langer and Applebee 1986, 1987; Langer 1995).

One of the most important features of a pedagogy designed to help students enter into culturally significant domains for conversation is that it invites genuine participation within the domain, the kind of participation that leads to knowledge-in-action rather than knowledge-out-of-context. At its best, such participation leads to what Csikszentmihalyi calls optimal experiences, in which people are so completely involved that they lose track of time and shut out everything but the activity itself. "It is what we feel when we read a well-crafted novel or play a good game of squash or take part in a stimulating conversation" (Csikszentmihalyi, Rathunde, and Whalen 1993, p. 14). Such experiences provide powerful opportunities for new learning, and the pleasure inherent in them convinces us that they are worth continuing to do for their own sake.

Optimal experiences are unlikely to be generated by the recitation activities that dominate many classrooms, in which students are quizzed about prior learning. They are more likely to occur in response to what Martin Nystrand and Adam Gamoran (1991, 1992) have called "authentic" questions, which encourage students to go beyond previous learning to explore new territory. In discussions that address authentic questions, meanings are expected to be negotiated in the course of discussion, the discourse is dialogic rather than monologic (Bakhtin 1981), and the outcomes emerge only as the discussion progresses. In their studies of literature and social studies teaching, Nystrand and Gamoran found that teachers ask very few authentic questions, but when they do ask such questions, students' learning is enhanced.

If questions are authentic, students are more likely to take interest in and derive satisfaction from their work. Changing the nature of the questions that are asked involves more than changing the form of the questions, however. It involves re-construing the underlying conventions governing discourse. The actual questions that a teacher asks are embedded in this larger context of expectations about what it means to partici-pate effectively in the class (and by implication, in the larger tradition that the class reflects). This larger set of expectations constitutes the meaning of any particular question that may be posed. Thus in some classes, "Why did Hamlet hesitate?" is a prompt for recitation of a previously presented interpreta-tion. In others, the same question may be an authentic invita-tion to explore possibilities, debate interpretations, and arrive at a new point of view. In the first case, the question taps students' knowledge of literature out of context; in the second, it invites students to participate in a tradition of literary study. Which expectation will prevail is determined by the purposes that have been established for classroom discourse, as well as the nature and direction of the disciplinary conversations into which students are expected to enter (Marshall, Smagorinsky, and Smith, 1995).

HELPING STUDENTS TAKE ACTION
ON THEIR OWN

The paradox of knowledge-in-action is that in order to learn something new, one must do what one doesn't yet know how to do. The way out of this paradox is to realize that learning is a social process: We can learn to do new things by doing them with others. Lev Vygotsky captured this insight when he argued (1962) that learning progresses from an *inter-* to an *intra-* psychological plane. Tomorrow we do on our own what today we do in the company of others.

In the classroom, the teacher is the critical mediator of that company. On the one hand, as I have already argued, the teacher mediates between the classroom and the larger tradition within which the classroom is embedded. This includes the tacit knowledge that shapes classroom discourse as well as the selections from the tradition that form the topics of discussion. With a teacher's guidance, we read and discuss what others have written, listen to what they have said, and in the process learn something about the tradition and how to formulate our own contributions to it.

The teacher also mediates among students within the classroom. The most obvious forms of mediation involve encouragement of direct collaboration: shared tasks and joint efforts that extend beyond what any of the collaborators could have accomplished alone. It also includes minor variations on collaboration, such as help or advice when stuck, responses to work in progress, or peer editing.

The activities that take place within classrooms have a didactic intent: By definition they occur because we want students to learn to enter into important cultural traditions of knowing and doing. Curricular domains are meant to be sites for learning, and therefore have a shape and structure that is planned rather than accidental. Like the classroom itself, the curriculum is a device for mediating between the students and the larger traditions that it reflects and embodies. Teachers enhance this mediating role in their selections of what to teach, their structuring of activities, and the standards of performance they encourage.

Csikszentmihalyi notes the delicate balance that effective teachers must strike between activities that are boring and those that are too demanding. When we ask students to enter into an intellectual tradition, to participate in a culturally significant domain for conversation, the kinds of contributions we expect must be appropriate to their level of knowledge and skills: Given the social nature of the model of learning I have been discussing, this means that we should seek the kinds of contributions that students could not do on their own, but can do with the help of others. This is what Vygotsky has called the zone of proximal development, where education can be most effective.

As Alan Purves has pointed out (1991), in the teaching of literature the level of appropriate difficulty is governed as much by the kinds of questions we ask as by qualities inherent in the texts we ask students to read. Texts can not only be read in many different ways, but as part of many different conversations. This is certainly true over historical time: We read and discuss many books long after the conversations that generated them have ended and the original participants have long been dead. It is also true for conversations that involve different participants at any given point in time. Thus in primary school classrooms, the poems of Robert Frost may be part of a conversation about capturing and sharing our experiences of people and places in our daily lives. In high school, the same poems may become part of a conversation about gender stereotyping or the development of the literature of New England. In college or graduate school, the same poems may be deconstructed as part of a conversation about the ways in which a group may define itself by whom it excludes from its discourse as much as by whom it includes.

Given the heterogeneous nature of American classrooms, the problem of finding the appropriate kind of participation for each individual might seem overwhelming. When questions are authentic, however, this difficulty is mitigated by the great latitude that most tasks have for redefinition by the participants. Just as books can be read in many different ways, what particular readers take from a book will vary depending on their purposes, knowledge, and previous experiences. In a similar way, students' own contributions to the conversation, whether written, oral, or embodied in other media, will reflect their current abilities to know and do within the tradition in which they are acting. To take a familiar though decontextualized example, a writing prompt such as ''Describe an interesting character'' can lead appropriately to a paragraph or two from a primary school student, a long essay from a high school student, and a *New Yorker* profile from a professional writer.

Students will negotiate their contributions in this way, however, only if the discussion conventions that have been established in fact treat everyone as having something interesting to contribute, and value the different contributions that everyone makes. The alternative, in which the same contribution is expected from everyone, ensures that virtually any activity will bore some students and frustrate others. Unfortunately, this is the situation in the many classrooms that treat learning as knowledge-out-of-context, emphasizing knowledge about, rather than participation in, significant traditions.

Teachers can also support students who are struggling to participate in new domains by helping them find appropriate structure for their activities. Some of that structure will come simply from the way the domain itself is specified: A curriculum is necessarily a selection out of a larger tradition of discourse, and as such is likely to be simpler and more orderly, with fewer contradictions and qualifications, than might be apparent in the domain as a whole. Thus an introductory science curriculum is likely to ignore the anomalies that Kuhn (1962/1970) argues accumulate at the edges of a paradigm, even though it is out of those anomalies that major advances in the field as a whole are likely to eventually occur. Students will find their own anomalies, however, that will in turn lead them to reformulate their own understanding.

Other structure is likely to reflect current understandings of the natural processes of thought and language that participation in the domain involves. The recent history of writing instruction provides a good example of how understandings of such processes can affect teaching and learning. As teachers in the 1970s began to conceive of writing as a set of processes of generating ideas, drafting, revising, editing, and sharing,[1] they began to reorganize classroom activities around their understanding of these processes. Some of the activities that entered the curriculum were new; others were familiar but reorchestrated in the service of the new image of what writers do.

---

1. A variety of overlapping terminologies have been used to describe the various strategies of writing; the list here is the one used by the National Assessment of Educational Progress.

(Outlining, for example, became a tool for revision instead of something that was always required before beginning to write.) These procedures (or strategies) in effect reorganized what students did when they wrote into a number of supporting activities that reflected our best understanding of natural processes of thought and language. Eventually, the typical pattern of activities in writing classrooms and writing textbooks began to reflect this reorganization (Applebee, Langer, Mullis, Latham, and Gentile 1994).

Judith Langer has similarly described (1990) the differing *stances* that readers take toward a text in the process of reading and understanding it. She uses the term *envisionment* to describe the text world that reflects a reader's current understanding, including all of the questions, hypotheses, and partial judgments that such understanding involves. Her stances include "being out and stepping into an envisionment"; "being in and moving through an envisionment"; "stepping back and rethinking what one knows"; and "stepping out and objectifying the experience." Each of her stances represents a strategy for making sense and elaborating meaning by drawing upon the reader's knowledge of the text and of the world. Like the strategies described in earlier studies of writing processes, Langer's stances are strategies readers use to enrich and elaborate meaning; they are recursive rather than linear, and together allow readers to elaborate on their understanding of what they are reading. In her collaborations with teachers, Langer (1991, 1995) then explored ways to help students enter into the various stances, and in turn to develop richer and more thoughtful envisionments of the texts they read and discussed. Taken as a whole, Langer's studies represent an attempt to better understand what constitutes natural processes of thought and language, and then to use that new understanding to more effectively help students enter into thoughtful discussions of literature.

The strategies that students learn in their reading, writing, and talk are socially constructed. They arise out of students' interactions with others within particular domains for knowing and doing, and in fact vary in their detail from one domain to another: A journalist writes in very different ways from a professor, and both differ from a politician. The strategies that are used to further conversation within a domain have another consequence: They not only provide models of how to complete particular types of tasks, but also models of how to learn to do new things. They are in effect socially constituted tools for learning to do things that have not been done before. My writing of this book can illustrate what I mean. Some of what I have been writing is well rehearsed: I have spoken and written about it before, in a variety of contexts. As a result, I have presentational routines that I can draw upon, ways of thinking about and presenting the material that allow the writing to go relatively smoothly and quickly. Other ideas are new for me; they represent explorations of implications that are, at least initially, quite unclear to me. I have no familiar routines to draw upon and hence I rely much more heavily on strategies for generating ideas, producing initial drafts, and revising in light of what I have written. Here my writing more closely resembles the kinds of approaches that are usually advocated by proponents of process-oriented writing instruction (myself included). These strategies of drafting and revision are particularly useful not because they represent "the way writers write." Rather they represent a set of strategies that writers have found to be useful when exploring ideas or genres or experiences that are new or unfamiliar. Such strategies in reading and writing are critical if traditions are to change and grow: They allow me to take actions and reach conclusions that have not been reached before.

COLLABORATION AND STANDARDS
OF ACCOMPLISHMENT

The teacher's role in helping students enter into domains for conversation is *essentially* collaborative; recent discussions of effective teaching have tried to capture this in metaphors such as "guiding," "mentoring," and "apprenticeship" (Rogoff 1990). Such metaphors emphasize the role of the teacher as providing support for the novice entering into a new domain, support that Judith Langer and I have analyzed as *instructional scaffolding* that enables students to accomplish in the context of the classroom what they could not accomplish alone (Applebee and Langer 1983; Langer and Applebee 1986, 1987; Langer 1991, 1995; Roberts and Langer 1991).

The notion of scaffolding is a useful analytic tool for describing the characteristics of classroom discourse that contribute to student learning. Interpreting scaffolding broadly, it can be seen in the way the domain is structured, in judgments about what activities are appropriate for a given group of students, in the orchestration of small-group, whole-class, and individual activities to introduce the knowledge necessary to complete tasks, and in the relationships between the activities that are undertaken and natural processes of thought and language. Scaffolding in the way we have used the term can be used to analyze all of the paraphernalia of instruction, from one-on-one discussion to textbook readings to whole-class and individual activities. All of these embody socially valued ways of knowing and doing that students will eventually internalize.

It is important, however, to remember that the scaffolding that may be present in any particular classroom reflects the teacher's and students' knowledge-in-action; it operates for the most part tacitly, shaping contributions during the press of ongoing interactions. As a pedagogical concept, scaffolding is most useful as a way for teachers to reflect on what they are doing, and on the nature of the environment for teaching and learning emerging in the classroom. It also provides a way to articulate and share what is happening with others, particularly with new teachers or with others who may be seeking to change their approaches to instruction.

When instruction is conceived as providing support for students' participation in significant conversational domains, the teacher's role changes from one of judging how well a student has performed to one of helping the student perform better. As Csikszentmihalyi describes it, teachers' contributions provide students with "that needed bit of knowledge essential to achieving a further step" (Csikszentmihalyi, Rathunde, and Whalen 1993, p. 192), rather than seeking to ensure that they reach a particular endpoint. Questions, partial apprehensions, false starts and new beginnings become part of the natural process of learning, encouraged and expected in reaching for new accomplishments.

At the same time, a classroom environment that encourages optimal experience requires high standards of accomplishment for each student. False starts must be treated as beginnings and not endings; misplaced goals must be reconstrued rather than rejected; partial knowledge must be challenged and extended. In a lively classroom environment in which real conversations are being engaged, this process of challenge and extension will be generated in part by the press of the conversation itself. Disagreement, divergent interpretations, alternative viewpoints should require participants to clarify and extend their own insights rather than capitulate to someone else's view. Teachers play a central role in ensuring that such high standards are always maintained. Through the questions they ask and the challenges they pose, effective teachers help students to focus, clarify, and raise the level of their contributions (Langer 1991, 1995; Roberts and Langer 1991). Although authentic questions may not have right answers, they do have more and less effective ways in which alternative answers can be proposed and defended.

ASSESSMENT

It has been very clear in recent years that systems of assessment have a profound effect on the nature of classroom teaching and learning. Examinations have effects that go far beyond the classroom. They classify students in relation to one another, and these classifications in turn affect the possibilities and opportunities that may be open to them. A middle school student who passes a test of basic competencies may go on to the high school; one who fails it may repeat the grade and turn down a path that will lead eventually to dropping out of school. A high school student ranked high in her class may win admission to a prestigious university that will in turn lead to advanced professional study; another ranked low may have to settle for a lesser-ranked college and a different career. Because the stakes can be high, students and teachers take exams seriously even when they question the value of what is assessed.

As I noted in chapter 3, much of the testing in American schools and colleges emphasizes knowledge-out-of-context instead of rewarding students' performances within culturally significant domains of knowing and doing. This situation has led to a variety of proposals for revising or abandoning tests as we know them. Among those proposals, the use of portfolios of student work has emerged as one of the most frequent and promising suggestions. Well-implemented portfolio assessments can ensure that assessment is aligned with curriculum, and that students are rewarded for their abilities to enter into the culturally significant domains for conversation around which the curriculum has been built. Portfolios do not guarantee salvation, however. They are simply a technology which can be put to use in many different ways. There is nothing inherent in the concept of portfolios, for example, that prohibits them from being used for demonstrations of knowledge-out-of-context. And in fact as portfolios have become more widespread, there have been suggestions to include some multiple-choice test samples to make it easier to calibrate performance across students and contexts. Though intended to answer some of the concerns about the psychometric characteristics of portfolio assessments, such suggestions will undercut the reasons for suggesting the use of portfolios in the first place.

There are, however, some examples of new systems of assessment at work. The Pacesetter project, discussed in the previous chapter, is experimenting with a variety of forms of portfolios and embedded assessments designed to provide information for instruction as well as accountability. In a related approach, Ted Sizer's Coalition of Essential Schools has instituted "exhibitions" of student work as part of the process of graduation. Modeled on earlier traditions of public examination, exhibitions represent a culmination of independent student work in a variety of conversational domains, shared in a public forum before public examiners at the end of a school career. Similarly, Arts Propel, a collaboration between Harvard University, the Rockefeller Foundation, and the Pittsburgh Public Schools, has developed a curriculum for the arts in which assessment is based on the results of students' engagement in long-term projects within the domains of the arts, rather than on demonstrations of knowledge-out-of-context (Wolf, Bixby, Glenn, and Gardner 1991). These projects are still young, however, and open to reevaluation and reconstrual; the particular configurations that their assessments take will evolve over time as they are implemented in new contexts.

Whatever the specific mechanisms may look like, the point here is that the kinds of performance that are rewarded in assessment must reinforce students' attempts to enter into culturally significant domains for conversation. This will mean that assessments must be based on knowledge-in-action—on students' demonstrations of their increasing mastery of valued systems of knowing and doing. This in turn will require us to articulate standards of performance in rather different ways than in the past. Simple demonstrations of "knowledge of" the subject will not be sufficient. Teachers and students will have to learn to look for additional indicators—in the ability to define interesting questions, to express a clear point of view, to gather evidence, and to structure arguments that are appropriate to the traditions to which students are seeking to contribute.

Toward a Unified System of Curriculum and Instruction

The changes in approaches to teaching and learning discussed in this chapter have been widely accepted in recent years, across a variety of subject areas. Education journals, conference programs, and textbooks for beginning teachers have emphasized the importance of helping students to think and reason on their own. States from New York to California have similarly revised their assessments and syllabi to encourage such approaches (see, for example, California State Department of Education 1987). Yet as I argued in chapter 3, classroom practice has responded much more slowly to such concerns. Recent reforms, in Cuban's now familiar metaphor (1984), have simply ruffled the surface of an unchanging ocean of traditional approaches.

In large measure, as I have been arguing in this book, the lack of responsiveness to new approaches has been the result of conceptions of curriculum that stress knowledge-out-of-context rather than knowledge-in-action. Such curricula lead naturally to the development of assessments that primarily reward memory and recitation, and these in turn lead teachers to emphasize such knowledge for the simple reason that it is essential to their students' success.

If curriculum is approached in terms of the significant conversations into which students are to enter, on the other hand, the emphasis from the beginning will be on knowledge-in-action. This in turn will lead to assessments that place their emphasis on students' developing abilities to enter into such conversations. Only at this point, with new approaches to curriculum driving new emphases in assessment, will we have created a unified system of curriculum and instruction, working together to help students enter into the rich traditions of knowledge-in-action that should be available to them as members of our diverse world.

nine

Reconciling Conflicting Traditions

Debates about curriculum are as much debates about the nature of the communities in which we live as they are debates about the traditions from which we come. The choices we make define the nature of our common culture—they institutionalize sets of values, codify social and political hierarchies, define the center and the periphery. In times and places of cultural conflict and social change, debates about curriculum are thus likely to become emotional and politicized. In the United States today this is most evident in discussions of such topics as multiculturalism and the teaching of values. Such topics challenge the balance among competing interests within the larger community and have the potential to fragment the political consensus upon which the American common school tradition rests: For when we cannot agree on what is legitimately a common curriculum, particular communities either seek refuge outside of the public system or seek to impose their values on the public system itself.

In discussing curriculum, it is important to recognize the many layers of values that are involved in curricular decisions. Some of these layers are easy to recognize, because they have been the focus of widespread debate. These include issues such as evolution versus creationism, the treatment of homosexual lifestyles, and sex education. Other layers of values are more subtle, embedded in the particular discourse conventions that govern how students will learn to make meaning within a given curriculum—in the kind of knowledge-in-action that the curriculum encourages. Goals for education that emphasize thoughtfulness and independent thinking treat discourse as open to alternative interpretations and meaning as relative.

For some communities within the United States, however, such a treatment of discourse runs counter to deeply held personal and religious convictions. Andrea Fishman, whose work (1988, 1990) was introduced in chapter 2, found that the Amish community she studied expected its schools to treat text as determinate and meanings as finite. Creativity and independent thinking were not appreciated. Deviation from these expectations on the part of a teacher who was herself Amish led to the teacher's dismissal.

James Moffett has also chronicled (1988) the depth of feeling that curricular choices can arouse, in his case in the context of Kanawha County, an Appalachian community in West Virginia. Faced with the adoption of textbooks that encouraged students to examine values and lifestyles, fundamentalist members of the community erupted in violence and anger. They saw the textbooks as a direct threat to their own religious beliefs, and to the authority of church and family. Car bombings, arson, and shootings ensued, schools closed, and the National Guard was eventually called in. The underlying cause of all the upheaval was, again, a real conflict between the discourse conventions—the traditions of knowing and doing— accepted by a sizable minority in the community and those reflected in the adopted curriculum.

When traditions of knowing are in conflict, educators are forced to recognize that the curricular choices they make reinforce one set of values at the expense of another. American schools are founded on premises of tolerance, diversity, nonsectarianism, and inclusiveness; they have characteristically stressed qualities of thoughtfulness, reflection, and independent thinking. Such characteristics, however, are themselves values that are not universally accepted within American society. Communities with traditions as diverse as those of Quakers, Roman Catholics, Hasidic Jews, Muslims, and Christian fundamentalists have so rejected the premises inherent in public education that they have founded their own independent schools and academies where their children can be educated in alternative traditions. (Curiously, private systems of education founded in rejection of the values of public education are sometimes proffered as models for public schools to emulate.)

The point in highlighting such conflicting traditions is to remind ourselves that the curriculum we provide is always value-laden. It is better to be aware of the values that underlie our curricular choices than to pretend that our choices are somehow value-free. The books we ask students to read, the issues we pose for discussion, and the patterns of independence and authority that we establish within our classrooms all reflect particular traditions of knowing and doing that are valorized by our choices, just as the less obvious decisions about books we exclude and issues we do not discuss marginalize or devalue other traditions.

EXCLUDED TRADITIONS

Critiques of curriculum over the past several decades have pointed out the extent to which the traditions introduced into American schools and colleges have been dominated by white, Anglo-European males, to the exclusion of women and of people from other ethnic and cultural traditions. (Elizabeth Minnich offers a good introduction to the argument in its general form [1990].) Such critiques have led to an extended series of projects to retrieve lost contributions and to reassess neglected ones. Proposals for curriculum reform have moved from simply adding neglected works to existing courses, to fundamentally reconstruing the basis of literary study to reflect the diversity of traditions in American culture (e.g., Lauter 1990; Greenblatt and Gunn 1992).

Arguments for a more representative curriculum have often been numeric: Women represent over half of our nation; non-white minorities are already the majority in some U.S. schools and soon will be in others. Though numeric arguments for representativeness can seem compelling, they have their own pitfalls, not the least of which is the fact that a strictly representational curriculum could end up being very narrow indeed. Sandra Stotsky, looking at population figures in the U.S.

(1994), argues that many minority groups (Native Americans, African Americans, and Eastern European Jewish Americans, for example) are already *over*represented in the curriculum, even as she argues in general for the need to include a broad spectrum of works reflecting the ethnic diversity and broad range of cross-cultural traditions in the United States. And she points out that 75 percent of the U.S. population traces its roots to Europe. Even works by women are vulnerable on a strictly representational argument, by a sleight of hand that shifts the focus from representation of the population at large to representation of published works from earlier historical periods (when women's access to channels of publication was limited and therefore works by women constituted a very small percentage of those available; see Reiss 1992).

There are better arguments for a more inclusive curriculum. All of us benefit from the breadth of vision and sensitivity that we gain through learning to enter into alternative systems of knowledge-in-action, including those represented by other literary and cultural traditions than our own. Isabel Allende, Toni Morrison, Naguib Mahfouz, Maxine Hong Kingston, Gabriel Garcia Marquez, Isaac Bashevis Singer, Ralph Ellison, Alice Walker, Gita Mehta—we read such authors not to satisfy some condition of numeric "representativeness" in our lives, but because they enrich our understanding of human diversities as well as commonalities—they expand the horizons of possibilities (Langer 1990, 1995) that we can envision, and thereby extend our range of understanding and ability to live in the world in which we find ourselves.

Another way to think about the role of literature is as a way of learning to make sense of the world. Implicit within a work of literature is a worldview that is the matrix out of which, and against which, the characters act. In a multicultural society, literature provides a mechanism for sharing alternative worldviews, making the inexplicable explicable, the uncommon common. Through literature, we may develop a basis for understanding acts and points of view that otherwise would simply be seen as deviant. We may even begin to understand that multiple voices in creative dialogue with one another are more typical than any single point of view (Bakhtin 1981).

As the curriculum is expanded to include a wider range of traditions, we confront a dilemma. On the one hand, these texts have a "repertoire" (Iser 1978; Earthman 1992) that will be less familiar, or even unfamiliar, to our students. Lacking the requisite background knowledge, they may be unable to make full sense of the texts, as even college freshmen in Earthman's study found when reading a short poem whose references were embedded in a Jewish tradition.

The quick reaction is that we must turn explicit attention to this missing background if we want the texts to be read and appreciated. The immediate danger with such an approach, however, is that this "background knowledge" can easily become a new knowledge-out-of-context, a more-or-less disembodied set of information to be taught and learned. Such a curriculum will re-create the worst features of the approaches it is designed to replace: the orientation toward correct interpretations of the New Criticism, and the overemphasis on historical and authorial context of the literary and cultural history that preceded it.

An alternative is possible, however, that relies on the reading itself to create a natural context for understanding (Dasenbrock 1992). That is, just as a novice entering any conversation will only gradually come to understand all of the nuances of the discussions under way, the novice in the multicultural arena will lack the depth of the more experienced reader. But in the process of reading more extensively, this depth will gradually be built up, and earlier works reinterpreted or even revisited with a new understanding. This is the way we gain knowledge-in-action in any arena, through gradual immersion in new conversations rather than by standing alongside and being told about them. Such an approach underlies Tony Harrison's multicultural approach to American literature in chapter 4, as well as Emily French's World Cultures class in chapter 5. It is also the basis of the Pacesetter English curriculum, discussed in chapter 6.

W. E. B. Du Bois, in *The Souls of Black Folk* (1903/1989), commented on the "double-consciousness" that came from being a black person in America: "One ever feels his two-ness,—an American, a Negro; two souls, two thoughts, two unreconciled strivings; two warring ideals in one dark body, whose dogged strength alone keeps it from being torn asunder" (p. 3). Houston Baker, Jr., has extended this notion in his discussion (1980) of the black American literary tradition—simultaneously positioned within and outside of the majority culture. That is, African-American authors have historically been in the position of being excluded from the majority culture, and yet at the same time have been dependent upon that culture to provide the major audience for their work. In part as a result, black discourse has developed unique layers of meaning that arise out of this simultaneous position within two cultures. Images and metaphors, as well as myths and stories as a whole, that are read one way within the majority culture may be read quite another way within the context of African-American experience; and for the knowledgeable reader, the two sets of meanings interact in complex and interesting ways. Baker traces the consequences of this doubleness across three hundred years from the colonial writings of Phillis Wheatley to the African nationalism of Amiri Baraka (né LeRoi Jones) in the sixties and seventies. In the preservation of African meanings and experiences, as well as in the exigencies of the heritage of slavery, Baker argues, there has been the "development of distinctive terms in a black encyclopedia of meanings. To bring all one knows to an understanding of the human condition is, for the black writer, to bring unique fields of meaning and value" (p. 122). In this sense of unique fields of meaning defined in the context of alternative traditions, the doubleness of the African-American vision is paradigmatic of the individual in a multicultural society: Situated within multiple traditions, the individual is always both insider and outsider, looking in on as well as out from a variety of traditions that may stand in uneasy relationship to one another.

In a multicultural society, we do not have the option of ignoring the voices around us, nor of imposing a single common cultural voice on them. Melting pot images of the United States have lost whatever relevance and power they may once have had, even though we may still debate what alternative should replace them. In such a society, curriculum must introduce students to diversity and multiple perspectives, seeking not consensus but understanding of difference, the willingness to listen, and the ability to disagree. As Maxine Greene has put it (1993), in our culture there are many different stories

> connected by the same need to make sense, to make meaning, to find a direction. . . . What is crucial is the provision of opportunities for telling all the diverse stories, for interpreting membership as well as ethnicity, for making inescapable the braids of experience woven into the fabric of America's plurality . . . the community many of us hope for now is not to be identified with conformity . . . , it is a community attentive to difference, open to the idea of plurality. Something life-affirming in diversity must be discovered and rediscovered, as what is held in common becomes always more many-faceted—open and inclusive, drawn to untapped possibility. (P. 17)

WHEN TRADITIONS COLLIDE

Mary Louise Pratt, reflecting on her experiences with a multicultural curriculum and a multicultural student body at Stanford University, has discussed (1991) the excitement and the exhaustion attendant on teaching and learning in the "contact zone" between alternative traditions. Confronting alternative sets of values, different ways of knowing and doing, can be threatening and stressful. Disagreements can be loud and emotions can run high as we learn to listen and understand what is being said from a different perspective. The outcome is likely to be the recognition of difference rather than the achievement of consensus. At their best, teaching and learning in the contact zone between traditions lead to understanding of where the "other" comes from, and the development of an ability to communicate across that difference (Dasenbrock

1992). (Understanding the origin of differences is not the same as endorsing a valueless relativism; we may still disagree with certain values and actions even though we understand they are deeply embedded in an alternative tradition.)

Literature offers both contact zones and safe houses. When we read within familiar traditions, we experience the comfort of the predictable. When we read in alternative traditions, we are asked to step into another perspective, to view the world from an unfamiliar tradition of knowing and doing. In so doing, we broaden the "great conversations" about literature and life that encompass our knowledge of humankind and the wisdom of the cultures that comprise it.

REPRISE: TOWARD A CURRICULUM OF KNOWLEDGE-IN-ACTION

In this book, I have argued that the knowledge that matters to individuals and to society is the knowledge-in-action that is learned through participation in living traditions of knowing and doing. In contrast, American education has long emphasized the knowledge-out-of-context that comes from studying about, rather than participating in, the traditions of discourse (literature, the arts, science, history, mathematics) that incorporate our past and provide tools for living in the present and approaching the future. In so doing, we have devalued and betrayed the very traditions that we seek to preserve.

This devaluation has been inadvert, an unexpected by-product of the ways that have been devised to plan and organize the very curricula that are meant to preserve the knowledge that matters: The inventories and analyses, the debates about what to teach and when, have stripped knowledge of the context that gives it life and vitality, and have produced curricula that leave students bored and teachers frustrated. As long as curriculum is thought about as knowledge-out-of-context, students will be assessed on such knowledge, and new approaches to teaching and learning will make little difference in what students learn.

Alternatively, curricula can be thought about as culturally

significant domains for conversation, and teaching and learning as the processes through which students become participants in those conversations. Such participation is a necessary step in transforming knowledge-out-of-context into knowledge-in-action. Through such conversations, students will learn not only the content that is important within each domain, but also the ways of thinking and doing that give that content life and vitality. They will learn to *do* science, for example, not just learn about its history and accomplishments; they will learn to solve problems and take action on their own.

Classroom discourse is the critical mediator between the conversation within the classroom and larger traditions of knowing and doing. Because curricular conversations are embedded in the larger traditions, learning to participate effectively in such conversations also involves learning what counts as effective evidence and argument in the larger traditions as well. Although classroom discussions may focus on different topics and go in different directions than those at the cutting edges of the field, they are part of the same broad enterprise; there is, as Carl Bereiter has pointed out (1994), no reason to treat them as different in kind.

Effective domains for conversation share a number of characteristics that were explored in earlier chapters. They center on language episodes of high quality; contain enough material to sustain extended discussion; focus on a set of interrelated experiences or ideas; and are carried out in a manner that helps students enter into the conversation. At their best they are integrated, so that ideas reflect forward and back on one another, allowing reconsideration and reconstrual as the conversation continues; such conversations provide students with the opportunity to most fully contextualize and explore the knowledge-in-action they gain from their curricular experiences.

A curriculum of conversations is more than just part of a pedagogy in support of knowledge-in-action, however. It also offers a way to think about the problems and possibilities of multiculturalism in our increasingly pluralistic world. Conversations have the possibility to be dialogic in Mikhail Bakhtin's

(1981) sense, allowing each voice to speak in all its uniqueness, and at the same time to be part of a larger whole: "I imagine this whole world to be something like an immense novel, multi-generic, multi-styled, mercilessly critical, soberly mocking, reflecting in all its fullness the heteroglossia and multiple voices of a given culture, people, and epoch" (p. 60). The image is very different from the melting pot, and suggests a way to imagine a common culture in which diversity yields richness rather than chaos.

The argument that underlies this book is rooted in two ongoing conversations, one about the nature of language learning and the other about curriculum. Both have long histories, and both have tried, unsuccessfully, to transform the nature of teaching and learning in our schools and colleges. I hope that in drawing upon both traditions, I have moved us closer to creating classrooms that are more interesting places in which to teach and to learn.

REFERENCES   • • • •

Adler, Mortimer J. 1940. *How to Read a Book: The Art of Getting a Liberal Education.* New York: Simon and Schuster.

———. 1952. *The Great Ideas, a Syntopicon of Great Books of the Western World.* Vols. 1 and 2. Great Books of the Western World, ed. Robert Maynard Hutchins. Chicago: Encyclopaedia Britannica, Inc.

Anderson, Richard C., Elfrieda Hiebert, Judith Scott, and Ian A. Wilkinson. 1984. *Becoming a Nation of Readers: A Report of the Commission on Reading.* Washington, D.C.: National Academy of Education.

Anderson, Ronald D., et al. 1994. *Issues of Curriculum Reform in Science, Mathematics, and Higher Order Thinking across the Disciplines.* Washington, D.C.: U.S. Government Printing Office for the Office of Research, U.S. Department of Education.

Applebee, Arthur N. 1974. *Tradition and Reform in the Teaching of English: A History.* Urbana, Ill.: National Council of Teachers of English.

———. 1977. "The Elements of Response to a Literary Work: What We Have Learned." *Research in the Teaching of English* 11 (Winter): 255–71.

———. 1978. *The Child's Concept of Story.* Chicago: University of Chicago Press.

———. 1984. *Contexts for Learning to Write: Studies of Secondary School Instruction.* Norwood, N.J.: Ablex.

———. 1986. "Problems in Process Approaches: Toward a Reconceptualization of Process Instruction." In *The Teaching of Writing,* edited by Anthony R. Petrosky and David Bartholomae. 95–113. Chicago: National Society for the Study of Education.

———. 1992. "Stability and Change in the High School Canon." *English Journal* 81:27–32.

———. 1993a. *Beyond the Lesson: Reconstruing Curriculum as a Domain for Culturally Significant Conversations.* Albany, N.Y.: National Research Center on Literature Teaching and Learning. Report 1.7.

———. 1993b. *Literature in the Secondary School: Studies of Curric-*

ulum and Instruction in the United States. Research Monograph No. 25. Urbana, Ill.: National Council of Teachers of English.

―――. 1994. "Toward Thoughtful Curriculum: Fostering Discipline-based Conversation." *English Journal* 83:45–52.

Applebee, Arthur N., Robert Burroughs, and Anita S. Stevens. 1994. *Shaping Conversations: A Study of Continuity and Coherence in High School Literature Curricula.* Albany, N.Y.: National Research Center on Literature Teaching and Learning. Report Series 1.11.

Applebee, Arthur N., and Judith A. Langer. 1983. "Instructional Scaffolding: Reading and Writing as Natural Language Activities." *Language Arts* 60:168–75.

Applebee, Arthur N., Judith A. Langer, Ina V. S. Mullis, Andrew S. Latham, and Claudia A. Gentile. 1994. *NAEP 1992 Writing Report Card.* Washington, D.C.: U.S. Government Printing Office for the National Center for Education Statistics, U.S. Department of Education.

Applebee, Arthur N., and Alan C. Purves. 1992. "Literature and the English Language Arts." In *Handbook of Curriculum Research,* edited by Phillip Jackson. 726–48. New York: Macmillan.

Arnold, Matthew. 1867/1961. *The Poetry and Criticism of Matthew Arnold,* edited by A. Dwight Culler. Boston: Houghton Mifflin.

Baker, Houston A., Jr. 1980. *The Journey Back: Issues in Black Literature and Criticism.* Chicago: University of Chicago Press.

Bakhtin, Mikhail M. 1981. *The Dialogic Imagination: Four Essays,* translated by Caryl Emerson and Michael Holquist. Austin: University of Texas Press.

Banks, James. 1993. "The Canon Debate, Knowledge Construction, and Multicultural Education." *Educational Researcher* 22:4–14.

Bennett, William J. 1988. *American Education: Making It Work.* Washington, D.C.: U.S. Department of Education.

Bereiter, Carl. 1994. "Implications of Postmodernism for Science, or, Science as Progressive Discourse." *Educational Psychologist* 29:3–12.

Berkenkotter, Carol, Thomas Huckin, and John Ackerman. 1988. "Conventions, Conversations, and the Writer: Case Study of a Student in a Rhetoric Ph.D. Program." *Research in the Teaching of English* 22:9–44.

Bloom, Allan. 1987. *The Closing of the American Mind.* New York: Simon and Schuster.

Bloom, Harold. 1973. *The Anxiety of Influence: A Theory of Poetry.* New York: Oxford University Press.

Blum-Kulka, Shoshana, and Catherine E. Snow. 1992. "Developing Autonomy for Tellers, Tales, and Telling in Family Narrative." *Journal of Narrative and Life History* 2:187–217.

Bobbitt, Franklin. 1918. *The Curriculum*. New York: Houghton Mifflin Co..

———. 1924. *How to Make a Curriculum*. New York: Houghton Mifflin.

Bogdan, Deanne. 1990. "Censorship, Identification, and the Poetics of Need." In *The Right to Literacy*, edited by Andrea A. Lunsford, Helene Moglen, and James Slevin. 128–47. New York: Modern Language Association.

Brody, Pamela, Carol DeMilo, and Alan C. Purves. 1989. *The Current State of Assessment in Literature*. Center for the Learning and Teaching of Literature. Report Series 3.1.

Brown, Rexford. 1991. *Schools of Thought*. San Francisco, Calif.: Jossey-Bass.

California State Department of Education. 1987. *English-language Arts Framework for California Public Schools, Kindergarten through Grade 12*. Sacramento: California State Department of Education.

Carey-Webb, Allen. 1993. "Racism and 'Huckleberry Finn': Censorship, Dialogue, and Change." *English Journal* 82:22–34.

Cassirer, Ernst. 1944. *An Essay on Man: An Introduction to a Philosophy of Human Culture*. New Haven: Yale University Press.

Castor, Betty, and Ann Reynolds (cochairs). 1994. *Pacesetter: An Essential Element in Realizing Educational Reform*. A Report of the National Commission on Integrated Standards, Teaching, and Assessment. New York: College Board.

Cazden, Courtney. 1979. "Peekaboo as an Instructional Model: Discourse Development at Home and at School." *Papers and Reports on Child Language Development* 17:1–19.

Cheney, Lynne V. 1994. "The End of History." *Wall Street Journal*, October 20.

Ciardi, John. 1960. *How Does a Poem Mean?* Boston: Houghton Mifflin.

Clapp, John Mantle (chair). 1926. *The Place of English in American Life*. Report of an Investigation by a Committee of the National Council of Teachers of English. Chicago: National Council of Teachers of English.

Cleveland, Charles D. 1849/1851. *A Compendium of English Literature, Chronologically Arranged, from Sir John Mandeville to William Cowper*. Philadelphia, Pa.: E. C. and J. Biddle.

Crusius, T. W. 1991. *Philosophical Hermeneutics*. Urbana, Ill.: National Council of Teachers of English.

Csikszentmihalyi, Mihaly, Kevin Rathunde, and Samuel Whalen. 1993. *Talented Teenagers*. New York: Cambridge University Press.

Cuban, Lawrence. 1984. *How Teachers Taught: Constancy and*

Change in American Classrooms, 1890–1980. White Plains, N.Y.: Longman.

Daniels, Harvey A. 1994. "Pacesetter English: Let Them Eat Standards." *English Journal* 83:44–49.

Dasenbrock, Reed Way. 1992. "Teaching Multicultural Literature." In *Understanding Others: Cultural and Cross-cultural Studies and the Teaching of Literature,* edited by Joseph Trimmer and Tilly Warnock. 35–46. Urbana, Ill.: National Council of Teachers of English.

DelFattore, Joan. 1992. *What Johnny Shouldn't Read: Textbook Censorship in America.* New Haven: Yale University Press.

Delpit, Lisa. 1986. "Skills and Other Dilemmas of a Progressive Black Educator." *Harvard Educational Review* 56:379–85.

———. 1988. "The Silenced Dialogue: Power and Pedagogy in Educating Other People's Children." *Harvard Educational Review* 58:280–98.

Dewey, John. 1899. *The School and Society.* Chicago: University of Chicago Press.

———. 1916. *Democracy and Education.* New York: Macmillan.

Du Bois, W. E. B. 1903/1989. *The Souls of Black Folk,* edited and with an introduction by Henry Louis Gates, Jr. New York: Bantam Classics.

Dyson, Ann Haas. 1984. "Learning to Write/Learning to Do School." *Research in the Teaching of English* 18:233–64.

———. 1993. *Social Worlds of Children Learning to Write in an Urban Primary School.* New York: Teachers College Press.

———. 1994. "Confronting the Split between 'the Child' and Children: Toward New Curricular Visions of the Child Writer." *English Education* 26:12–28.

Earthman, Elise. 1992. "Readers' Literary Processes." *Research in the Teaching of English* 26:351–82.

Eeds, Maryann, and Deborah Wells. 1989. "Grand Conversations: An Exploration of Meaning Construction in Literature Study Groups." *Research in the Teaching of English* 23:4–29.

Eisner, Elliot W. 1982. *Cognition and Curriculum: A Basis for Deciding What to Teach.* New York: Longman.

Elbow, Peter. 1990. *What Is English?* New York: Modern Language Association.

Elias, Kristina. 1994. "A Positive Look at Pacesetter English." *English Journal* 83:50–53.

Elliott, David L., and Arthur Woodward. 1990. "Textbooks, Curriculum, and School Improvement." In *Textbooks and Schooling in the United States,* edited by David L. Elliott and Arthur Woodward. 223–32. Chicago: National Society for the Study of Education.

Erskine, John. 1948. *My Life as a Teacher*. Philadelphia: J. B. Lippincott.

Fetterley, Judith. 1978. *The Resisting Reader: A Feminist Approach to American Fiction*. Bloomington: Indiana University Press.

Feyerabend, Paul K. 1975. *Against Method: Outlines of an Anarchistic Theory of Knowledge*. Atlantic Highlands, N.J.: Humanities Press.

Fishman, Andrea R. 1988. *Amish Literacy: What and How It Means*. Portsmouth, N.H.: Heinemann.

———. 1990. "Becoming Literate: A Lesson from the Amish." In *The Right to Literacy,* edited by Andrea A. Lunsford, Helene Moglen, and James Slevin. 29–38. New York: Modern Language Association.

Gates, Henry Louis, Jr. 1992. *Loose Canons: Notes on the Culture Wars*. New York: Oxford University Press.

Goldenberg, Claude. 1992/93. "Instructional Conversations: Promoting Comprehension through Discussion." *Reading Teacher* 46: 316–26.

Gombrich, Ernst H. 1968. *Art and Illusion*. London: Phaidon Press.

Graff, Gerald. 1987. *Professing Literature: An Institutional History*. Chicago: University of Chicago Press.

———. 1992. *Beyond the Culture Wars: How Teaching the Conflicts Can Revitalize American Education*. New York: W. W. Norton.

Greenblatt, Stephen, and Giles Gunn, editors. 1992. *Redrawing the Boundaries: The Transformation of English and American Literary Studies*. New York: Modern Language Association.

Greene, Maxine. 1993. "The Passions of Pluralism: Multiculturalism and the Expanding Community." *American Educational Research Journal* 22:13–18.

Grice, H. P. 1975. "Logic and Conversation." In *Syntax and Semantics,* vol. 3, edited by P. Cole and J. L. Morgan. 41–58. New York: Seminar Press.

Gugliotta, Guy. 1994. "Up in Arms about the 'American Experience.'" *Washington Post,* October 28, A3.

Halliday, Michael A. K. 1977. *Learning How to Mean*. New York: Elsevier.

Harris, Charles B. 1988. "Canonical Variation and the English Curriculum." *ADE Bulletin* No. 90: 30–43.

Harris, Wendell V. 1994. "What Is Literary History?" *College English* 56:434–51.

Hatfield, W. Wilbur (chair). 1935. *An Experience Curriculum in English*. A Report of the Curriculum Commission. New York: D. Appleton–Century Co.

Heath, Shirley Brice. 1983. *Ways with Words*. New York: Cambridge University Press.

Herrington, Anne. 1985. "Writing in Academic Settings: A Study of the Contexts for Writing in Two College Chemical Engineering Courses." *Research in the Teaching of English* 19:331–61.

Hillocks, George, Jr. 1986. *Research on Written Composition*. Urbana, Ill.: National Conference on Research in English.

Hirsch, E. D., Jr. 1987. *Cultural Literacy: What Every American Needs to Know*. Boston: Houghton Mifflin.

Hirsch, E. D., Jr., Joseph F. Kett, and James Trefil. 1988. *The Dictionary of Cultural Literacy*. Boston: Houghton Mifflin.

Holzman, Michael. 1995. "Pacesetter English: Now That We're All Here, What Do We Do?" *English Journal* 84 (January): 77–79.

Huber, Bettina J. 1992. "Today's Literature Classroom: Findings from the MLA's 1990 Survey of Upper Division Courses." *ADE Bulletin* 101 (Spring): 36–60.

Huber, Bettina J., and David Laurence. 1989. "Report on the 1984–85 Survey of the English Sample: General Education Requirements in English and the English Major." *ADE Bulletin* No. 93: 30–43.

Hutchins, Robert M. 1952. *The Great Conversation: The Substance of a Liberal Education*. Vol. 1. Great Books of the Western World, edited by Robert Maynard Hutchins. Chicago: Encyclopaedia Britannica, Inc.

International Reading Association and the National Council of Teachers of English. 1989. *Cases in Literacy: An Agenda for Discussion*. Newark, Del.: International Reading Association and the National Council of Teachers of English.

Iser, Wolfgang. 1978. *The Act of Reading*. Baltimore: Johns Hopkins University Press.

Kuhn, Thomas S. 1962/1970. *The Structure of Scientific Revolutions*, 2d ed. Chicago: University of Chicago Press.

Langer, Judith A. 1987. "A Sociocognitive Perspective on Literacy." In *Language, Literacy, and Culture: Issues of Society and Schooling*, edited by Judith A. Langer. 1–20. Norwood, N.J.: Ablex.

———. 1990. "The Process of Understanding: Reading for Literary and Informative Purposes." *Research in the Teaching of English* 24:229–60.

———. 1991. *Literary Understanding and Literature Instruction*. Albany, N.Y.: National Research Center on Literature Teaching and Learning. Report 2.11.

———. 1992. "Speaking of Knowing: Conceptions of Knowing in the Academic Disciplines." In *Writing, Teaching, and Learning in the Disciplines*, edited by Ann Herrington and Charles Moran. 69–85. New York: Modern Language Association.

———. 1995. *Envisioning Literature: Literary Understanding and Literature Instruction*. New York: Teachers College Press.

Langer, Judith A., and Arthur N. Applebee. 1986. "Reading and Writing Instruction: Toward a Theory of Teaching and Learning." *Review of Research in Education* 13:171–94.

———. 1987. *How Writing Shapes Thinking: A Study of Teaching and Learning*. Research Monograph Series No. 22. Urbana, Ill.: National Council of Teachers of English.

Langer, Judith A., Arthur N. Applebee, Ina V. S. Mullis, and Mary Foertsch. 1990. *Learning to Read in American Schools: Instruction and Achievement in 1988 at Grades 4, 8, and 12*. Princeton, N.J.: National Assessment of Educational Progress.

Langer, Susanne K. 1942/1969. *Philosophy in a New Key*. Cambridge, Mass.: Harvard University Press.

Latour, Bruno. 1987. *Science in Action*. Cambridge, Mass.: Harvard University Press.

Lauter, Paul. 1990. "The Literatures of America: A Comparative Discipline." In *Redefining American Literary History,* edited by A. LaVonne Brown Ruoff and Jerry W. Ward, Jr. 9–34. New York: Modern Language Association.

Levine, Lawrence W. 1988. *Highbrow/Lowbrow: The Emergence of Cultural Hierarchy in America*. Cambridge, Mass.: Harvard University Press.

Lipson, Marjorie Y., Sheila W. Valencia, Karen K. Wixson, and Charles W. Peters. 1993. "Integration and Thematic Teaching: Integration to Improve Teaching and Learning." *Language Arts* 70:252–63.

Lloyd-Jones, Richard, and Andrea Lunsford. 1989. *English Coalition Conference: Democracy through Language*. Urbana, Ill.: National Council of Teachers of English.

Lynch, James J., and Bertrand Evans. 1963. *High School English Textbooks: A Critical Examination*. Boston: Little, Brown.

Marshall, James D., Peter Smagorinsky, and Michael Smith. 1995. *The Language of Interpretation: Patterns of Discourse in Discussions of Literature*. NCTE Research Report No. 27. Urbana, Ill.: National Council of Teachers of English.

Martinez, Miriam G., and William H. Teale. 1993. "Teacher Storybook Reading Style: A Comparison of Six Teachers." *Research in the Teaching of English* 27:175–99.

Mayher, John S. 1990. *Uncommon Sense: Theoretical Practice in Language Education*. Portsmouth, N.H.: Boynton/Cook.

McCarthy, Lucille P. 1987. "A Stranger in Strange Lands: A College Student Writing across the Curriculum." *Research in the Teaching of English* 21:233–65.

McGill-Franzen, Anne, and Cynthia Lanford. 1994. *Exposing the Edge of the Preschool Curriculum: Teachers' Talk about Text and Children's Literary Understandings*. Albany, N.Y.: National Research Center on Literature Teaching and Learning. Report No. 2.21.

Mersand, Joseph. 1960. "The Teaching of Literature in American High Schools: 1865–1900." In *Perspectives on English,* edited by Robert C. Pooley. 269–302. New York: Appleton-Century-Crofts, Inc.

Milanés, Cecilia Rodrigues. 1992. "Racism and the Marvelous Real." In *Social Issues in the English Classroom,* edited by C. Mark Hurlbert and Samuel Totten. 246–57. Urbana, Ill.: National Council of Teachers of English.

Minnich, Elizabeth K. 1990. *Transforming Knowledge.* Philadelphia, Pa.: Temple University Press.

Moffett, James. 1988. *Storm in the Mountains: A Case Study of Censorship, Conflict, and Consciousness.* Carbondale: Southern Illinois University Press.

Nash, Gary B., and Charlotte Crabtree. 1994. "A History of All the People Isn't PC." *Wall Street Journal,* November 21, A17.

Nystrand, Martin, and Adam Gamoran. 1991. "Instructional Discourse, Student Engagement, and Literature Achievement." *Research in the Teaching of English* 25:261–90.

———. 1992. "From Discourse Communities to Interpretive Communities." In *Exploring Texts: The Role of Discussion and Writing in the Teaching and Learning of Literature,* edited by George Newell and Russel Durst. 91–112. Norwood, Mass.: Christopher-Gordon.

Opie, Iona, and Peter Opie. 1959. *The Lore and Language of Schoolchildren.* Oxford: Oxford University Press.

Palincsar, Annemarie S., and Ann L. Brown. 1984. "Reciprocal Teaching of Comprehension-fostering and Monitoring Activities." *Cognition and Instruction* 1:117–75.

Polanyi, Michael. 1958. *Personal Knowledge.* London: Routledge and Kegan Paul.

Powell, Arthur G., Eleanor Farrar, and David K. Cohen. 1985. *The Shopping Mall High School: Winners and Losers in the Educational Marketplace.* Boston, Mass.: Houghton Mifflin.

Pratt, Mary Louise. 1991. "Arts of the Contact Zone." *Profession* 91:33–40.

Prior, Paul. 1994. "Response, Revision, Disciplinarity: A Microhistory of a Dissertation Prospectus in Sociology." *Written Communication* 11:483–533.

Purves, Alan C. 1973. *Literature Education in Ten Countries.* Stockholm: Almquist and Wiksell.

———. 1991. "Indeterminate Texts, Responsive Readers, and the Idea of Difficulty in Literature." In *The Idea of Difficulty in Litera-*

ture, edited by Alan C. Purves. 157–70. Albany: State University of New York Press.

———. 1992. "Testing Literature." In *Literature Instruction: A Focus on Student Response,* edited by Judith A. Langer. 19–34. Urbana, Ill.: National Council of Teachers of English.

———. 1993. "The Ideology of Canons and Cultural Concerns in the Literature Curriculum." In *Multicultural Literature and Literacies,* edited by Suzanne M. Miller and Barbara McCaskill. 105–27. Albany: State University of New York Press.

Reiss, Timothy J. 1992. *The Meaning of Literature.* Ithaca, N.Y.: Cornell University Press.

Roberts, Doralyn, and Judith A. Langer. 1991. *Supporting the Process of Literary Understanding: Analysis of a Classroom Discussion.* Albany, N.Y.: National Research Center on Literature Teaching and Learning. Report 2.15.

Rogoff, Barbara. 1990. *Apprenticeship in Thinking: Cognitive Development in Social Context.* New York: Oxford University Press.

Rogoff, Barbara, and William Gardner. 1984. "Adult Guidance of Cognitive Development." In *Everyday Cognition,* edited by Barbara Rogoff and James Lave. 95–116. Cambridge, Mass.: Harvard University Press.

Rosenberg, Warren. 1990. " 'Professor, Why Are You Wasting Our Time?': Teaching Jacob's Incidents in the Life of a Slave Girl." In *Conversations: Contemporary Critical Theory and the Teaching of Literature,* edited by Charles Moran and Elizabeth F. Penfield. 132–48. Urbana, Ill.: National Council of Teachers of English.

Rosenblatt, Louise M. 1978. *The Reader, the Text, the Poem.* Carbondale: Southern Illinois University Press.

Russell, David R. 1991. *Writing in the Academic Disciplines, 1870–1990: A Curricular History.* Carbondale: Southern Illinois University Press.

Scholes, Robert. 1985. *Textual Power: Literary Theory and the Teaching of English.* New Haven: Yale University Press.

———. 1991. "A Flock of Cultures—A Trivial Proposal." *College English* 53:759–72.

———. 1995. "An Overview of Pacesetter English." *English Journal* 84 (January): 69–75.

Seixas, Peter. 1993. "The Community of Inquiry as a Basis for Knowledge and Learning: The Case of History." *American Educational Research Journal* 30:305–24.

Shaw, Peter. 1994. *Recovering American Literature.* Chicago: Ivan R. Dee.

Shulman, Lee. 1987. "Knowledge and Teaching: Foundations of the New Reform." *Harvard Educational Review* 57:1–22.

Silva, Cecilia, and Ester L. Delgado-Larocco. 1993. "Facilitating Learning through Interconnections: A Concept Approach to Core Literature Units." *Language Arts* 70:469–74.

Smith, Dora V. 1932. *Instruction in English*. Bureau of Education Bulletin 1932, no. 17. Washington, D.C.: U.S. Government Printing Office.

———. 1941. *Evaluating Instruction in Secondary School English*. A Report of a Division of the New York Regents' Inquiry into the Character and Cost of Public Education in New York State. Chicago: National Council of Teachers of English.

Spivey, Nancy N. 1990. "Transforming Texts: Constructive Processes in Reading and Writing." *Written Communication* 7: 256–87.

Stotsky, Sandra. 1994. "Academic Guidelines for Selecting Multiethnic and Multicultural Literature." *English Journal* 83:27–34.

Tharp, Roland G., and Ronald Gallimore. 1988. *Rousing Minds to Life: Teaching, Learning, and Schooling in Social Context*. Cambridge, U.K.: Cambridge University Press.

Tyack, David, and William Tobin. 1994. "The 'Grammar' of Schooling: Why Has It Been So Hard to Change?" *American Educational Research Journal* 31 (Fall): 453–79.

Van Doren, Mark. 1943. *Liberal Education*. New York: Henry Holt and Co.

Villanueva, Victor, Jr. 1993. *Bootstraps: From an American Academic of Color*. Urbana, Ill.: National Council of Teachers of English.

Vopat, Jim. 1995. "A Nomination for the 1995 Doublespeak Award." *English Journal* 84 (January): 80–82.

Vygotsky, Lev S. 1962. *Thought and Language*. Cambridge, Mass.: M.I.T. Press.

Wall Street Journal. 1995. "Senate Rescues History." January 19, A18.

Waller, Gary F. 1986. "A Powerful Silence: 'Theory' in the English Major." *ADE Bulletin* No. 85: 31–35.

Walmsley, Sean A. 1994. *Children Exploring Their World: Theme Teaching in Elementary School*. Portsmouth, N.H.: Heinemann.

Weeks, Ruth Mary (chair). 1936. *A Correlated Curriculum*. New York: D. Appleton–Century Co.

Wells, Gordon, and Gen Ling Chang-Wells. 1992. *Constructing Knowledge Together: Classrooms as Centers of Inquiry and Literacy*. Portsmouth, N.H.: Heinemann.

Wineburg, Samuel S. 1991. "On the Reading of Historical Texts: Notes on the Breach between School and Academy." *American Educational Research Journal* 28:495–519.

Wolf, Dennie Palmer. 1995. "Of Courses: The Pacesetter Initiative and the Need for Curriculum-based School Reform." *English Journal* 84 (January): 60–68.

Wolf, Dennie Palmer, Janet Bixby, John Glenn III, and Howard Gardner. 1991. "To Use Their Minds Well: Investigating New Forms of Student Assessment." *Review of Research in Education* 17:31–74.

Wolf, Shelby Ann, and Shirley Brice Heath. 1992. *The Braid of Literature*. Cambridge, Mass.: Harvard University Press.

INDEX

• • • •